A Compelling Passion...

D0034099

CALLED TO
SERVE

The
KEN COX
STORY

KENNETH COX
WITH JOLENA KING

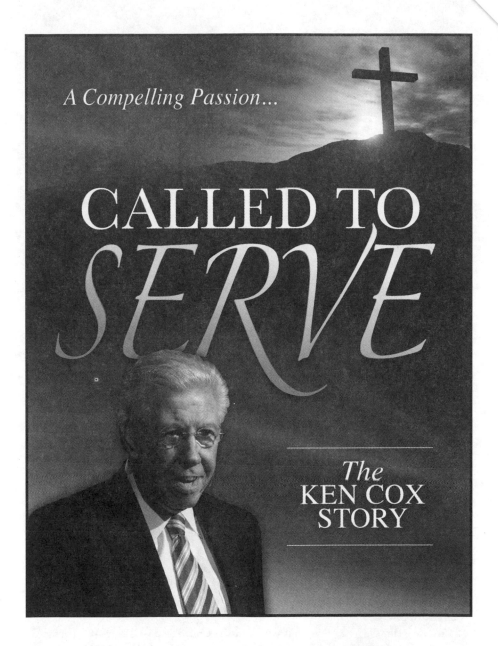

A Compelling Passion...

CALLED TO *SERVE*

The
KEN COX
STORY

3ABN
3ABN BOOKS

P. O. Box 220
West Frankfort, Illinois
www.3ABN.org

Pacific Press® Publishing Association
Nampa, Idaho
Oshawa, Ontario, Canada
www.pacificpress.com

Edited by Bobby Davis
Cover design by Crystique Neibauer
Cover image from Shutterstock.com
Inside photos provided by Kenneth Cox
Inside design by Aaron Troia

Copyright © 2010 by Pacific Press® Publishing Association
Printed in the United States of America
All rights reserved

The author assumes all responsibility for the accuracy of all facts and quotations as cited in this book.

Scripture quotations marked KJV are from the King James Version of the Bible.

Scripture quotations marked NIV are from the HOLY BIBLE, NEW INTERNATIONAL VERSION®. Copyright © 1973, 1978, 1984 by International Bible Society. Used by permission of Zondervan Publishing House. All rights reserved.

Scriptures quoted from NKJV are from The New King James Version, copyright © 1979, 1980, 1982, Thomas Nelson, Inc., Publishers.

You can obtain additional copies of this book by calling toll-free 1-800-765-6955 or by visiting http://www.adventistbookcenter.com.

3ABN BOOKS is dedicated to bringing you the best in published materials consistent with the mission of Three Angels Broadcasting Network. Our goal is to uplift Jesus Christ through books, audio, and video materials by our family of 3ABN presenters. Our in-depth Bible study guides, devotionals, biographies, and lifestyle materials promote whole person health and the mending of broken people. For more information, call 618-627-4651 or visit 3ABN's Web site: www.3ABN.org.

Library of Congress Cataloging-in-Publication Data:
Cox, Kenneth, 1934–
  Called to serve : the Ken Cox story / Kenneth Cox with Jolena King.
    p. cm.
  ISBN 13: 978-0-8163-2390-6 (pbk.)
  ISBN 10: 0-8163-2390-9 (pbk.)
  1. Cox, Kenneth, 1934– 2. Seventh-day Adventists—United States—Clergy—Biography.
  3. Evangelists—United States—Biography. I. King, Jolena Taylor, 1940– II. Title.
  BX6193.C68A3 2010
  269'.2092—dc22
  [B]

2010002407

10 11 12 13 14 • 5 4 3 2 1

Dedication

This book is dedicated to my wife, Marilyn, who God, in His mercy and love, lent me for a short while. She helped me, encouraged me, understood and shared my desire, and inspired me in my walk with the Lord. Her selfless dedication as a wife and mother was enhanced by her love for the Lord. With what kind and tender words she touched our lives. As it says in her favorite song, "If I have wounded any soul today, please Lord, forgive." She brought a little bit of heaven to this earth, enriching my life and many others by being here.

Acknowledgments

Thank you, Bobby Davis, for the countless hours in refining and making it personal. Kay Kuzma, you were truly a blessing. Thanks for your insight and encouragement. I'm indebted to my daughter, Laura Becker. Thank you for helping me remember the events and their order. To my sisters, Billie Day and Dorothy Morgan, for your help with the early days of our lives. Team members: Thank you, Dona Klein, for listening and helping me make the sentences readable. Diane Loer and Lindi McDougal, thank you for your editorial work.

Contents

Introduction

Why write this book?

Because I have a compelling passion to reach you—the man, woman, or young person who feels that you've been handed a situation in life that isn't fair. Perhaps you've felt disadvantaged because of an illness, or perhaps you were raised in a part of the country where you couldn't get the education others received. Perhaps you didn't have the necessities of life because of your financial condition, or perhaps you have suffered verbal and physical abuse.

These are the things that I've faced in life. They could have easily caused me to think, *Well, it's no use. I can't make it.* But this story is about how Christ can take anyone who will turn his or her life over to Him and drastically change that life—no matter how poor, sick, beat down, or uneducated that person may be.

No, the change doesn't happen instantly. It takes time. There are lots of ups and downs, plenty of mistakes, and a tremendous amount of growing pains. We live in a world of sin and disease, so inevitably there will be heartache and loss. There will be areas in which God will ask you to step out of your comfort zone, and you'll feel totally inadequate. But that's how you'll learn to depend on Him.

God has a purpose for you, and He will supply your every need in this journey with Him. My great desire is that you will read this book and find the hope and strength I've found in Jesus Christ.

Then my life—and this book—will not have been in vain!

* * * * *

When anyone sets out to record the events that shaped their lives, God's guidance may be very obvious in one instance, while it may appear questionable in another. We humans are on a planet claimed by the enemy of souls, but our great God overrules in human affairs in various ways and for reasons of His own. He owes us no explanations, and we are left to trust Him—regardless. Or not. (See Job 38–41.) That God can and will use a mortal man or woman for His divine purpose is totally a result of His amazing grace.

This book is about how God's hand has been over my life— sometimes welcome and clearly seen through joy, fulfillment, success, and contentment; at other times veiled and hard to understand in separation through death, disappointment, discouragement, and tears. God took a Chicago urchin—an Oklahoma farm boy, a failure in school—and allowed him a small role in spreading the gospel of Jesus Christ during these last days. What mercy and what grace!

May you, dear reader, be able to see God's mercy, His grace, and His guiding hand in these pages—as well as in your own life.

Kenneth Cox

Chapter 1

An Unforgettable Christmas

I will never leave thee, nor forsake thee.
—Hebrews 13:5, KJV

I remember the first time I learned about Mama's headaches. It was Christmas Day. I was four. The reason I remember that Christmas so well is that Donald and I had tied our big toes together with a string the night before so neither of us could get up without waking the other. Of course, every time one of us moved, it awakened us both—so it had been a long night. Before we went to bed, we had gone through Dad's drawer and located his largest socks. Already an expert on Christmas, I knew they would be bulging the next morning with nuts and candy.

A cold wind whistled past the windows of our one-bedroom flat as the weak sun peeked over the tenement row houses. I was out of bed in a flash, jerking my big brother's toe before I remembered the string.

The commotion woke up the entire family. Even if we had tried, we couldn't have gotten out of the room without waking Dad and Mama in one bed and our sisters in the other.

"Wow, Dorothy, look at this!" I shrieked as I ran to the Christmas tree in the living room, pulling out a doll in a blanket from the top of the brightly wrapped gifts.

Still rubbing her eyes, my two-year-old sister came over and grabbed

Left to right: Donald, Dorothy, Otto, Laura, Kenneth, and Billie

her new baby, embracing the soft bundle in her arms.

"Oh, look! *Look!*" my big brother Donald and I squealed in unison as we spotted our wooden trucks—a fire engine with real ladders and wheels and a logging truck with a trailer-load of logs.

"Thank you! Thank you!" we kept saying, sharing our toys and playing together as my parents and older sister, Billie, sat watching us.

"When will Uncle Virgil and Aunt Sally get here?" seven-year-old Donald asked.

"Oh, not long—maybe a couple of hours. Everyone else will be here too," Mama said. "Come on, Billie, I need your help in the kitchen."

As she began to stand up, her hand shot to her head.

"Oh! Oh! Ow! *My head! Oooo,* it hurts," she said, sinking back down into the sofa.

Panic stricken, I watched Mama sit motionless for a moment, tears streaming down her face.

"Oh, Otto, I've never had a headache like this!" she groaned to my dad. "I don't have time for this now, but I can't even stand up!"

Realizing this was serious, my dad took charge. "Laura, don't get up. Just rest. It'll probably go away. We'll cancel Christmas dinner. Billie, bring your mother some water while I go find some aspirin and call the doctor. Here, Laura, lie down and relax."

She protested weakly, saying all she needed was to rest for a few minutes. As she did, we were sent, wide-eyed, to the bedroom. *What is happening to my mama?* I wondered. *Why is she crying?* We tried not to think about it as we sat on the bed and talked quietly.

Forty-five minutes later, Mama got up slowly, and four sets of young eyes watched Dad walk her to the kitchen. He stood around helplessly until she ordered him to leave and go help us straighten up the house.

I kept glancing back at Mama as she carefully removed from the icebox the food that she and Billie had been cooking for the past few days. Although quieter than usual, she seemed to be OK as she placed food in the oven, lit the gas burner, and began setting the table.

Laura Cox

A ticking bomb

A year went by, and Mama suffered increasingly frequent dizzy spells and headaches, frequently needing to steady herself by gripping whatever piece of furniture was close by. Finally, she visited a doctor, who told her that she had an iron deficiency, but the iron pills and extra liver she ate didn't seem to help much.

Because we were so young, my siblings and I weren't very concerned. Sometimes Billie would send us down to the basement to play or tell us to be quiet so Mama could rest. But none of us realized the seriousness of what was happening.

One day Mama came down with flulike symptoms, and because her regular physician was out of town, Billie and Dad took her across the street to a young doctor instead. He examined her carefully and used a small light to look into her eyes.

"You have a tumor in your eye," he said, clearly alarmed. "It's large enough that I see it, and I'm afraid it's a ticking time bomb! I want you to go to the hospital as soon as you can."

Billie was gripped with fear. She was old enough to understand that the situation was serious, and her mind raced through several scenarios.

The X-rays they took at Chicago's Cook County Hospital confirmed the doctor's diagnosis. Not only did she have a tumor on her optical nerve, but a huge brain tumor as well.

If there is a God . . .

Dad paced the floor outside the waiting room as he reviewed the events of the past few weeks. Mama's headaches had become almost constant, and she obviously had needed surgery. Through an unusual "coincidence," the young doctor she had seen had mentioned her case to his mentor, Dr. Adrien Verbrugghen, the famous neurosurgeon.

After examining her, Dr. Verbrugghen had offered to remove the massive and unusual brain tumor at no cost in the name of medical research. Dad knew he would still have to pay the hospital bill, but he would take on a third job, if necessary.

Now his heart was gripped with fear. *If there is a God out there, this would be a good time for You to show up!*

My parents were nominal Christians. They took us to church occasionally, typically at Easter or Christmas, but that was about it. I'm sure Dad wondered whether Mother would survive this delicate and invasive procedure. What if she wasn't "right" afterward? How would he manage alone with four children?

After eight long hours, Dr. Verbrugghen called him out of the waiting room. He explained that although the surgery was fairly successful, he'd been able to only remove half the tumor because it was wrapped around some important nerve centers in Mama's brain. With more room in her skull, he hoped that the tumor would now loosen its grip, allowing him to remove the rest of it in a second, more invasive surgery a few months later.

Dad thought it best not to tell Mama about the second surgery right away, and the doctor deferred to his judgment.

Alone with her thoughts

In a few days, Mama was moved from the intensive care unit into a semiprivate room near the nurses' station. Her pain had eased considerably, and she missed us. Dad had come by every afternoon on his way home from work, but we children hadn't been allowed to visit Mama.

Because her roommate was incoherent and had few visitors, Mama spent a lot of lonely time reflecting on her life, marriage, children, and her illness. Dr. Verbrugghen had suggested that perhaps the tumor had been the result of the bad fall she'd suffered when she was twelve. Already she felt amazingly better, though. Surely she would soon be able to get back to her home and family and resume her life.

Poor Billie, only sixteen, was already doing the work of a mother: shopping, cooking, cleaning, and tending to the younger ones. She rarely complained and was so dependable.

Unfortunately, Mama had lost her second child, Jogene, to double pneumonia, just as he was developing his winsome, happy personality. Now he was resting in an Oklahoma cemetery.

Donald was her little mechanic who could take apart and put together almost anything. Well, let's just say that he was much better at taking things apart! Clever and cheerful, he was a natural leader too.

But he certainly didn't come with an instruction manual!

I had come next—so tiny for my age and afflicted with asthma when I was only eighteen months old. I talked and dreamed of running and playing with other kids, but no matter how much I wanted to, I dared not. It was hard enough to breathe when I stood still.

Our financial situation meant limited medical treatment, so Mama and Dad learned to be resourceful in treating my condition. Sometimes in the evenings, they would gather us up for a ride as I gasped desperately for my next breath. Before inhalers, I seemed to get the most relief by hanging my head out the window as we drove down the streets—even in the dead of winter!

Then there was Dorothy, always compliant, and maybe just a tiny bit spoiled as the baby of the family. She always seemed intuitively aware of the needs of others—*compassionate* was the best way to describe her. Dorothy and I were fast friends and fiercely protective of each other!

Dad hadn't seemed overjoyed when any of us were born, but he had been noticeably distant with Dorothy and me. Now, looking out the window at the cold, gray skies, Mama must have longed to move back to Oklahoma. It had been so hard to leave the fresh air, green fields, and meadows for the dark, smoky, and crowded streets of Chicago; but when the coal mines closed in 1928, they had no choice. Dad had searched unsuccessfully for a job near home. Then Mama's brothers wrote, telling that work was plentiful in Chicago. Reluctantly, after burying Jogene, our parents packed everything and moved to the big city.

It wasn't all bad, though, Mama told herself. *What a blessing it had been for Otto to have a regular job during the Great Depression!* She'd seen the lines of people waiting for government handouts; she knew that if they'd stayed in Oklahoma, they'd have been in a similar line too.

Growing up poor

Chicago, Illinois, was not a good place to raise a family—at least not in our neighborhood in 1934, the year I was born. Gangsters ran the city streets as the Great Depression brought about a massive migration of people looking for jobs.

Our neighbors included people of Irish, Polish, and German backgrounds. The tenements we lived in were narrow, several stories

Grandparents Fate and Annie Hankins

tall, and only two feet apart. Although we children weren't allowed to play in the street, we could run free in the back alley.

Traditional toys were hard to come by, and one of our *favorite* pastimes was to push around small iron rims, up and down the alleys with sticks. We also loved to bat things around, and any object would do. I still have a scar on my forehead from a tin can that was destined to become a home run, but managed to hit me instead! Trucks would back up to the coal chute in the alley and disgorge their contents into our basement. The whole process fascinated me, and I'll never forget the day I got a whipping for coming into the house covered in coal dust from standing too close to the chute!

Dad worked hard to provide for his family, though it wasn't easy to keep food on the table for four kids. He and Mama managed the tenement building we lived in, renting out the upstairs flats. Eventually, they even moved into the basement so they could rent out their own flat for a little more cash.

Dad would get up at 2:00 A.M. during the winter months to go down to the docks to unload grocery cargo until almost daylight. Then he would rush home, grab his lunchbox, and head to his job at the Wyckoff Steel Mill. The grueling manual labor and long hours took their toll on him physically, and I believe they took their toll on his attitude as well. My parents were used to hard work, though. Both of them grew up on farms in Oklahoma.

Grandparents Fate and Annie Hankins

My mother was part English and Choctaw Native American. Her parents, Grandma and Grandpa Hankins, lived on a twenty-acre truck farm in a four-room house with a kitchen, a living room, and two bedrooms. The old woodstove in the kitchen provided the only heat source in the house. I remember Grandpa Hankins didn't have a car; his horse and wagon provided their transportation.

Mama enjoyed being near her parents, so every other summer she would pack us up and take us to the farm. We would grow a big garden, can lots of vegetables and fruits, and often attend Sunday School and church. We loved milking cows, churning butter, and snatching fresh eggs from under the hens.

Left to right: Mother Laura, Dorothy, Kenneth, Donald, and Billie

Grandma, bless her soul, dipped snuff—a polite way of saying she chewed tobacco. In my mind's eye, I can still see the coffee cans in every corner of the living room—and her incredible aim as she spit tobacco juice and saliva across the room. I never once saw her miss a can!

I wasn't born yet when my paternal grandmother died, but I do remember Grandpa Larkin Cox. He was German and Irish, and he was a mean man! He evidently made a lot of enemies, too, because he plowed his fields with a cigar box containing his revolver strapped between the plow handles. My dad told me that when he was a young lad, his father offered him fifty cents if he could pick a certain number of pounds of cotton in one day. After working feverishly, without a break all day, he finally met his goal and proudly accepted the prize money. But the next morning, his father told him that he dared not pick one pound less from that day on—with no reward, of course.

Mama told me many years later that when I was a tiny two-year-old, my crying upset Grandpa so much he walked into the room and slapped me clean off my high chair onto the floor!

Mama's recovery

Billie had been bossing us around all morning, no doubt wondering how she'd gotten stuck with all that responsibility, when Dad's '34 Plymouth pulled up out front. We all rushed to the window. Mama was back from the hospital!

My brother thought Mama looked bad, but Billie made sure he understood he was only to compliment her. Her head was covered with bandages, and her face looked puffy, but as soon as she was in the door, we crowded around her, full of questions.

No, her head wasn't hurting like it used to, but it still hurt some because of the surgery.

Yes, they'd shaved her head, but a little stubble was already growing back.

"It's really good to be home and to see every one of you, but I'm so tired!" she said. "Do you mind if I go to bed for a while?"

Dad and Billie helped her to the bedroom, and when they came out, Dad closed the door behind him. He looked serious, and in his stern way, he explained how we'd have to play quietly for the next few days.

"All of you must be nurses to help your mother get well," he said. "I'm heading back to work in the morning, and Billie's in charge when I'm gone. And you'd better do whatever she says, or I'll take care of you when I get home at night! Understand?"

We nodded solemnly, and although we didn't like Billie bossing us around, we fully understood the consequences of not obeying Dad!

Mama's recovery was far more rapid than expected, and Billie wasn't nearly as bossy as we'd feared.

Chapter 2

The World Explodes

When I am afraid, I will trust in you.
—Psalm 56:3, NIV

Six months had passed since her operation, and Mama was feeling so good she'd already made several shopping trips to Macy's—and it was only the first week of December! We'd heard her singing in the bedroom as she wrapped presents, but on Saturday morning, she had a bit of a headache and felt rather dizzy. Not wanting to alarm us, she decided to simply take it easy to see if the strange feeling would go away. *Surely the tumor can't be back already!* she reasoned. *Christmas is only three weeks away—why spoil it for everyone?*

The next day the unthinkable happened. As news spread that Japan had bombed Pearl Harbor, a dark pall of fear fell over the land. More than two thousand lives had been lost, and a brutal blow had been dealt to the country's pride. America's hands-off policy in the world came to an immediate end as President Roosevelt called up the entire United States military and officially declared war. Patriotism ran at an all-time high, and eligible young men volunteered for the armed forces in droves. Hospitals gave up doctors, nurses, and materials for the cause. Soon many factories closed from the shortages of raw material, while new ones opened to supply the troops. Americans were angry at the Japanese and uneasy about their own safety. Armageddon seemed just around the corner!

Dorothy and I were too young to understand what everyone was talking about, of course. All we knew was that Mama didn't seem sick anymore, and that made our little world a good place to be. But a couple of weeks after Christmas, Billie awoke to loud voices and crying coming from the living room.

"I'm sorry, Laura! I am so sorry," Dad was saying.

"Why didn't you tell me sooner that I'd have to have more surgery?"

"I just wanted you to enjoy the time in between, Laura. Think how good it's been for the last few months! Could you have felt that way if you'd known?"

"Otto, are you saying I might die in surgery?" There was fear in Mama's voice. "Are you saying I might not be OK afterward?"

Dad tried in vain to reassure Mama. While the tumor didn't seem to be malignant, she could not afford to skip the surgery either.

A major setback

Dr. Verbrugghen got right to the point when he came out of surgery. Things hadn't gone as well as he'd hoped. Although Mama's vital signs were good, he was afraid there might have been some residual nerve damage and that some motor skills may have been affected. He also told Dad he'd never seen such an invasive benign tumor and that it was amazing she'd been feeling as well as she had.

"We think she might have had a mild stroke while under the anesthesia," he said, "but she's a fighter, and I believe she'll recover as well as anyone could. And, oh yes, at one point during the surgery, her tongue blocked her airway, and we had to do an emergency tracheotomy to keep her breathing."

It all seemed like a bad dream to Dad. He had expected that Mama would again recover quickly and that the tumor and her illness would be forever gone. Several hours passed before he was allowed to see her, and when he did, he was not prepared for what he saw.

She looked close to death—pale skin, an IV, and tubes seemingly everywhere. She appeared to be asleep and at first didn't respond when he called her name. Then her eyes fluttered and opened—at least her left eye did. Her right eye opened only halfway. As she tried to smile, he noticed that the right side of her face was drooping.

He reached for her right hand. It was cold and unresponsive.

"How ya doin'?" he asked, but he couldn't make out the garbled response.

Trying to swallow the lump in his throat, he suddenly realized that his beautiful thirty-six-year-old wife would be an invalid for the rest of her life. *What will I tell the children? How can our family manage?*

"I'll be back later," he said, patting her arm. "Must go see about the kids, you know. You be good now and rest."

Once he was far enough down the hall, Dad began cursing. "All right, God! Where are You now? Just where *are* You?" A tirade of profanity followed that would have made a sailor blush. Walking outside, he headed straight for a bar.

Nurses were no longer plentiful at the hospital—many were now serving in the military. One night someone opened the window just before the shift ended and forgot to close it. The Chicago night air in January was bitterly cold, and, predictably, Mama came down with pneumonia and was very ill for a number of days. When she recovered sufficiently, she came home in a wheelchair. She was paralyzed on her right side, blind in her right eye, and deaf in her right ear. But even more devastating to her was the fact that her once-beautiful face was now distorted, sagging, and disfigured.

Once again we gathered around the window as Donald helped Dad lift her wheelchair up the front steps—with her in it. We watched in stunned silence as they rolled her into the living room.

"Mama, I'm glad you're home," Dorothy said, giving the wheelchair a hug. And although no one mentioned her sagging face, Mama felt our wondering stares.

"I'm hungry," Dad said, trying to get past the awkward moment. "Got any food cooked?"

"Yes," Billie answered, "there's food on the stove, Dad. Mama, can you feed yourself, or do you need help?"

"I think tho," she answered with a slur. "I been prac-ti-thing."

Asthma attacks

This time Mama's recovery was long and slow. She was determined to walk again, to care for her family, and to speak properly. But one problem impeded her progress more than any other—she hated the way she looked, and she figured Dad must feel the same way. Trips to the doctor's office were now a major ordeal. If he so much as spoke to the nurse, Mama thought he was being enticed by the nurse's charms. She assumed that Dad was flirting constantly because now every woman was "more attractive" than she was. Jealousy reared its ugly head and attacked with vengeance, and Mama seemed unable to control her vicious accusations, even though they were obviously driving him further and further away. Sadly, the rift in their relationship was noticeable even to us.

Dad then decided to move us back to Oklahoma—God's country, he called it. We had experienced too much sadness in the big city, where houses were jammed together and clear skies and breezes were rare. The fresh air and the nearness to her parents might help Mama get better, and it might help her not be so paranoid. But the dream had to be deferred. Due to her many handicaps, we had to postpone the move, but Donald, who was now thirteen, begged to go help Grandma and Grandpa Hankins and to live with them during the following school year. Meanwhile, my seventeen-year-old sister, Billie, had fallen in love, and by that Christmas, she was married.

Life suddenly became very busy for Dorothy and me as we scrambled to fill the void our big brother and sister had left. Fortunately, Billie didn't live far away and would often stop in to help.

By the end of 1942, Mama was able to get around on her own inside the house, using the wheelchair only for outside excursions. But try as we might, Dad wasn't happy with Dorothy and me. He expected us to do the work of four children—plus take care of our mother. In his eyes, we were hopelessly inadequate.

"Can't you two do anything right?" he would yell, adding a few curse words for good measure. "I've never seen such stupidity!" Buried in his own problems, he was blind to the effect his harsh words and actions had on his nine-year-old son and six-year-old daughter.

After Dad's raging verbal attacks, my asthma would also rage, but I dared not let anyone but Dorothy know I had made that connection. He would surely have seen it as a sign of weakness. My asthma attacks rendered me immobile for a couple of hours—or even all night—gasping, wheezing, and fighting to draw in every breath. I remained extremely small for my age, and even Dorothy began to outgrow me.

At last, in the summer of 1943, we made the big move. We said Goodbye to our tenement house, and Dad put Mama and her wheelchair on the train to Oklahoma, with Dorothy and me instructed to take care of her every need. He would follow later in the car, after he sold as many of our household belongings as he could.

I was scared. The air on the train was thick with cigarette smoke, and I could feel a serious asthma attack on the way. But I had to be strong for Mama and Dorothy. After all, I was the man of the family on this trip. Fortunately, I was able to find a seat by an open window.

Chapter 3

Growing Up Okie

They cannot fathom what God has done from beginning to end.
—Ecclesiastes 3:11, NIV

We hardly recognized the young man who met us at the train station in Oklahoma! Donald had grown, his voice had deepened, and his speech was really strange! His strong Oklahoma accent sounded funny to me, and I didn't understand his odd phrases. In a few months, though, I developed the same "Okie" accent—a malady that would remain with me for life!

What a delightful change Oklahoma was. I had traded sidewalks, streets, and tenement row houses for meadows, woods, and wide-open spaces. Most of all, I loved having the freedom to explore! However, there were some things I had to get used to. Our farmhouse had no running water, so, of course, we had to run and get it. We also had no indoor toilet.

Our large garden produced abundantly—but it had to be worked

Kenneth and Donald

Kenneth and Donald

and picked and canned. Mother cooked on a woodstove, and that stove had a huge appetite for wood. It also served as the only source of heat in the house. Our bedroom doors were kept closed in the winter so we could keep the rest of the house warm. A skinny kid, I would crawl into bed on cold winter nights between sheets that felt just like ice! I'd lie shaking in one spot until I got it warm—and then I didn't dare move for the rest of the night!

From left to right: Donald, Roscoe, Kenneth, and Dorothy

When Dad arrived in Oklahoma, one of the first jobs he tackled was to dig a well—which still provides water to this day. Together we cultivated the twenty-acre truck farm in addition to the other jobs he worked to make ends meet. Because I was so small for my age, Dad had me use a Georgia stock, or grub plow, to break up the soil in the furrows between the plants. It was a light plow, and if it hit a rock, it would pop out of the ground and hit the corn before I could stop it! I knew I'd get a whipping as soon as Dad found out, so I tried very hard to watch for rocks and hold the plow steady, repairing any damage as quickly and quietly as I could when I did have an accident! Sometimes Dad would send me out to hoe in the garden, but as a nine-year-old I had a hard time keeping my weeds straight. Young okra and young cockleburs look just alike, and I knew that if I chopped the wrong plants with my hoe, I was in *big trouble*!

In spite of this, life on the farm was lots of fun. I loved animals and thoroughly enjoyed riding a horse without a saddle or bridle. Off we'd go through the fields as I leaned in close, tapping one side of its neck to make it turn, or saying "Whoa" to slow it down.

One day Dad took us with him to buy a new horse. I'd never seen such a beautiful animal! Prince was coal-black, handsomely built, and had rippling muscles down his forelegs.

"Donald, you go ahead and ride him home," Dad said.

I wish he'd told me I could ride! Why does Donald get to have all the fun? I wondered.

Back at the house, I anxiously awaited them in the yard. They seemed to take forever, but finally I could see them coming down the lane.

"Let me ride! Please let me ride!" I begged, jumping up and down.

Dad picked me up and swung me up on the horse behind my brother. Prince immediately began pitching, snorting, and bucking, and in a few seconds, both of us were on the ground.

"Are you hurt?" Dad asked, picking us up and dusting us off.

Nothing was injured, of course—except our pride, which lay there in the dirt where we'd landed. Dad seemed surprised because he'd been told that Prince was a gentle horse.

"Donald, get back on," he ordered.

"Dad!" he protested, but up he went. Prince was as calm as could be. Then Dad swung himself up, too, and immediately the horse began snorting, pitching, and bucking until both Dad and Donald were on the ground!

It was quite a show, and Dad called the horse everything but nice. I didn't dare laugh, though. Prince had made his point: he was always happy to take one person for a ride, but would never allow two people on his back.

Behind the coal house

We attended the little Lone Oak country school about a mile away. Each of the three rooms held three or four grades. Shortly after I started attending, I overheard the boys in my room whispering about going behind the coal house during recess. I was often left out of whatever the other kids were doing because of my asthma, so I followed the boys, desperate to fit in.

Paul pulled out a folded tobacco leaf that had been twisted and dried, taking a bite out of it and handing it to the next boy. He took a bite of the twist tobacco, too, and passed it my way. Determined not to be left

Lone Oak School, now used as a hay barn

27

out, I bit off a plug and started chewing it, but by the time recess was over, I felt very sick.

"Hey, look at Kenneth!" Ruben said, laughing. "His face is purple!"

And he was right! They'd all chewed tobacco long enough so they didn't even have to spit it out when they went back into the classroom. But my stomach was churning, and my head was spinning as I put my head on the desk and closed my eyes.

"Ruben, are you chewing?" Mrs. Lewis asked.

Ruben swallowed his tobacco plug in one gulp, innocently answering in the same breath, "No, Mrs. Lewis."

Before she could ask me what was wrong, I raised my hand, "Mrs. Lewis, I'm sick. May I go home?"

The next day we were back behind the coal house again, and I didn't have sense enough not to go.

"We're sorry we made you sick," they apologized. "When school got out yesterday we went to town and bought you some special beechnut tobacco. You can handle this kind."

Giving in to peer pressure, I tried it again and soon learned to chew tobacco right along with the rest of them. Later, in high school, I also started smoking. Never mind the asthma—healthful living was not a consideration when it came to fitting in!

Put-downs

In spite of never hearing him say so, I always knew Dad loved us. Mother was the more approachable parent. But hugs and kisses were not part of our family's emotional language.

My dad was hard. We children were often hit about the head and sometimes whipped with the razor strop that hung behind the door. Dad never lifted a hand to my mother, as far as I know, but worse than the physical abuse was the verbal abuse we all suffered. I remember him saying, "If your brains were nitroglycerin, you wouldn't have enough to blow your nose!" Such put-downs hurt me all my life—

until I met Jesus Christ. It was only then that I was able to put them behind me and accept that I was a child of God, as was my dad. I was then able to focus my life on Jesus.

There was no denying his temper toward Dorothy and me—especially following Mother's second operation and the onset of her jealous outbursts. After we moved to Oklahoma, Donald wasn't home much, so it fell to me to "help" when Dad was doing anything mechanical.

"Kenneth, bring me a ten-inch crescent wrench," he would call from under the car. I'd run to the toolbox and begin searching, but nothing said "crescent wrench" on it.

"Do you know where it is, Dad?"

"Kenneth, it's right over there on the workbench!" he'd say, adding some choice cusswords.

That workbench looked twenty feet long! *Where would a crescent wrench be?* I wondered. Then, as I searched feverishly for the tool, I'd hear Dad coming out from under the car.

"Can't you find nothin'?" he'd yell, backing up his question with more foul language. The next thing I knew, I was being hit about the ears, back, bottom, and legs.

"Get out of here! You're no help at all!" he'd rage, literally picking me up and throwing me to the ground.

I despaired of ever learning all I needed to know to please my father. I had no one to turn to. We attended church only occasionally, and the thought of a heavenly Father didn't even cross my mind. I believe He must have watched all this with deep sadness.

Baptized—for all the wrong reasons

When I was ten, our minister gathered all the children who were roughly my age.

"Now boys and girls, it is time for you to be baptized," he said. "If you are ready to take that step—and every one of you should be—please sign up on this piece of paper. We'll have a baptism on June eleven, and you'll need to have your parents sign one of these consent forms."

Nothing was mentioned about accepting Jesus Christ as our Savior or what we should believe in order to participate in this sacred rite.

I was baptized right along with the rest of the kids my age.

Driving lesson

Since I was very young, I'd been longing to learn how to drive, and by the time I was twelve, that desire was overwhelming.

"I know how to drive now!" I repeatedly told my father after driving the car around the yard a few times.

One of his jobs was driving a school bus, and one day, when our family's old Plymouth simply wouldn't start, Dad drove his school bus out of the yard and chained the car behind it.

"OK, Kenneth," he said, "now's your chance! Get in the car, turn on the ignition, push down on the clutch, and put the car in first gear. Keep the clutch in, and I'm gonna pull you. Once you start moving, just let the clutch out slowly while you give it some gas."

When he was satisfied that I understood what to do, he began pulling me down the road behind that big bus. I let out the clutch—and the car started!

Whoa!

It startled me so much that I immediately shoved the clutch back in. Then I let it out again, pushing hard on the gas pedal. The car lurched forward and slammed into the school bus, hitting it hard enough to bounce back on its chain tether!

Flustered, I pushed in the clutch again, and let it out, giving the car more gas. And, of course, it rammed the bus a second time! By the time the bus and the car came to a halt, both headlights were shattered and dangling, both fenders were severely dented, and the grill was knocked into the radiator!

I jumped out of the driver's seat and hung my head, trembling and cowering in fear.

I peeked up at Dad as he came walking back to me. He looked ten feet tall, and he was shaking his head and muttering. He looked at the car, then bent down and silently unhooked the chain from the bus.

"All right! Get back in and drive it home," he said in a strained, terse voice. "You can't possibly hurt it any more than you already have!"

Fishing with Dad

"Kenneth, get your fishing gear ready," Dad said one evening when he came home from work. "I'll ask Mother to fix us a lunch, and tomorrow when I get off work, we'll go spend the night on the Kiamichi River to do some fishing!"

It was such fun to be out there by the river—just Dad and me. He walked over to some post oak trees—so called because they're often used to make fence posts. The trees often put out two- or three-foot-long shoots from their base, and now he cut off a few and made a lean-to.

"If you get tired, you can take a nap here," he said, spreading out a blanket underneath.

I slipped an earthworm over the hook, cast it into the water, and sat down. I waited a while, but the fish weren't biting. Soon I was bored, so I walked over to the lean-to and lay down on the blanket, ready for a nap. Suddenly, a flash of lightning streaked across the horizon, and the rumble of thunder followed. Part of the region nicknamed "Tornado Alley," Oklahoma is famous for violent storms that develop very quickly.

The thunderstorm came closer, and finally Dad came and sat down beside me. As the storm passed over our little shelter, the thunder shook the ground beneath us—seemingly re-adjusting the rhythm of our hearts! The lightning was so brilliant, I could still see it through my tightly closed eyes.

I still recall that storm every time I hear the text describing the Lord's coming, "For as lightning that comes from the east is visible even in the west, so will be the coming of the Son of Man" (Matthew 24:27, NIV).

Roscoe, the "benched-legged" dog

Dad was a good hunter and was also good at teaching dogs to hunt. They were used for hunting squirrels and raccoons, but the dogs were absolutely forbidden to chase rabbits. In fact, they were so well trained that rabbits could play in front of them and they'd just lie there without even barking!

"Otto, some cockeyed critter hit my henhouse twice last week, and last night he got a pig!" It was my Uncle Horace, and he was "madder 'n hornets," as the locals would say. "I'm aimin' to go after him tonight. You wanna go?"

"Yeah, I'll go with you. Where do you think it is? In the woods behind your place?"

"Most likely."

"Dad! Dad!" I said, a pleading look on my face. And so it was that my little mixed-breed puppy, Roscoe, and I tagged along on the great nighttime hunting expedition!

Roscoe was just a little short-haired, reddish-colored pup with oddly bent hind legs (benched-legged, in Oklahoma jargon), but with him by my side, I felt like one of the big boys!

Our hunting party walked a long way into the woods before black-

Otto Cox

ness settled around us, the men's carbide headlamps projecting a path of light before us. Suddenly, the older hunting dogs started barking and running, and there was a terrific scurrying in the brush! Surrounding a nearby tree, they barked furiously.

"Quick! Shine your light up there, Horace! Let's see what we've got!"

"Well I'll be, Otto. That's sure 'nuf one big bobcat! Look at the size of him!"

I could see the bobcat, eyes gleaming and muscles tensing as he crouched lower on the limb, as Roscoe whimpered and pressed up against my leg. Dad took careful aim with his rifle and pulled the trigger. The bobcat tumbled out of the tree and fell with a thud into the underbrush.

With that, the dogs darted toward the downed cat, Uncle Horace right behind them.

Surprise! The bobcat sprang up on all fours and took after Uncle Horace!

What a sight that was—Uncle Horace, six feet tall and running like ninety—with that cat right behind him! Luckily, the injured cat didn't run far before stumbling and falling lifeless to the ground. This time he really was dead.

Uncle Horace finally relaxed enough to chuckle with Dad and me. After a couple of minutes, he picked up the dead animal and threw it over his shoulders, holding it by its hind feet. That cat was so large that its front feet hit the calf of my uncle's left leg!

As the night wore on, my puppy and I became tired, lagging farther and farther behind.

"Kenneth, are you coming?" Dad said impatiently, turning around and shining his light my direction. Then he swore.

"Look at *that!*"

His light had picked up what appeared to be scores of tiny lights beaming back at him. A large pack of wolves was only a few feet behind me, following the bobcat's trail of blood. Immediately, they began to howl!

Dad kept his loaded gun cocked and on his shoulder the rest of the way home, just in case the wolves became more aggressive. Needless to say, Roscoe and I walked ahead of the men for the rest of the trip—and we didn't have any trouble staying awake or walking fast, either!

Choctaw beer

Jones Academy, a school for young Choctaw Indian boys was two miles from our home, and from time to time, our high school in Hartshorne would participate in intramural sports such as basketball, baseball, and boxing. Because of the Choctaw influence in the community, a lot of the families made a home brew they called Choctaw beer. They usually kept it in their cellars, which made it generally accessible to young boys like me.

At times my buddies and I would help ourselves from someone's cellar and spend the night fishing and drinking. Of course, we often got drunk and participated in more than our share of foolishness too. Because Mother and Dad didn't place many restrictions on us, we didn't have to be home at any certain time at night. This nonchalant attitude obviously wasn't very beneficial to our character development.

"Ya better be here in time to milk the cows in the mornin'!" was all Dad would say.

Often, as teens, Donald and I would come in very late—or very early in the morning. I always tried to be careful not to wake anyone up, tiptoeing in quietly with the lights off.

"Kenneth, is that you?" Mother would ask every time. She did the same with Donald. She knew us by our footsteps alone.

The idea of having a beer was not something that was given much thought, since my dad and all my uncles drank. At times they even gave us a drink. Underage drinking was not frowned on in our part of the world.

Another loss

In November of 1948, my baby brother, William David, was born at home, but soon it became evident that something was seriously wrong. After rushing him to the hospital, the doctors discovered that the massive blood transfusions Mother had received during her second surgery had sensitized her blood to the Rh factor. Too late they discovered that her antibodies had damaged her unborn baby, and he lived only a few days. It was a very sad time for us as we laid little William's body to rest near his brother, Jogene.

By the next summer, though, things seemed almost back to normal. Not only had Mother emotionally endured the loss of her baby, she had, by sheer determination, made a significant recovery from her brain surgery as well.

Chapter 4

A Horse Called Blue

It is of the LORD's mercies that we are not consumed, because his compassions fail not. They are new every morning: great is thy faithfulness.
—*Lamentations 3:22, 23, KJV*

Dad seemed to be feeling unusually generous that day, just as I was about to turn fourteen.

"Kenneth, your birthday's comin' up the end of this month, and your mother thinks you might like to have a colt of your own. Whaddaya think?"

"Are you serious? *Of course* I'd love to have my own colt! When can we get him? May I break him myself?"

Dad knew someone who had a young colt for sale at a reasonable (very low) price, so within a few days, Blue was in our barn. This was the best present I ever could have dreamed of having, and I loved him from the moment I saw him. I fed, watered, and curried him every day for a year. Soon Blue would be big enough to begin breaking in. We were inseparable, and I thought his bluish-gray color was incredibly distinctive. There were never enough hours in a day to spend all the time I wanted with him.

I broke him. He wasn't hard to break at all. I can remember there was no problem. I crawled on his back, and he was a little skittish. But I don't remember him pitching or bucking. There was a real bond between us.

In June the long summer of canning began. Although Mother had improved tremendously, she was still unable to stand for very long.

Kenneth

And besides, she was making all the tedious preparation of all the fruits and vegetables. There were hundreds of jars in the cellar that had to be brought upstairs and washed. Since I had the only strong hands in the family that would fit inside a quart jar, it fell to me to wash them all.

I felt abused. After all, I was almost fifteen, and the more I thought about it, the more unjust the situation looked. *This is women's work, and besides, the mold in the cellar and the dust on the jars is hard on my asthma!* No sooner did I get one boxful washed than twenty more boxes were waiting in the cellar! First, it was enduring my dad's beatings when I didn't measure up, and now my mother was abusing me! *I'm not appreciated here at all,* I thought. *I'll just leave, and then we'll see how they get along without me!*

Runaway

Don had married and was living in Bakersfield, California, so I decided to run away from home and go live with him. I had no money, of course, but why would a fourteen-year-old need money? I had no idea what the world outside of my little Oklahoma town was like.

Leaving with only the clothes on my back, I slept by the side of the road the first night. But God's protective hand was over me, even though I didn't know it, and the next morning, a nice older couple stopped their car for me.

"Need a lift?"

"Sure do. You goin' toward California?"

"Will Arizona help?"

"Sure!" I said, as I climbed into the backseat.

"I believe there's still some food back there if you're hungry," the lady said. "Just look in that basket."

I was starved, and the fried chicken was gone in no time!

I was lucky on my first ride, but the second one scared me half to death! Suffice it to say

Donald, Otto, and Kenneth

that only the Lord saved me from that unsavory character, and I was lucky to be alive. But halfway across the country already, there was no turning back. Luckily, my next ride took me all the way to San Bernardino, California, but it was nighttime when I was dropped off in the middle of town—160 miles away from my brother's place! As I walked down the street, wondering where I was, a policeman pulled up beside me.

"Where you headed, son?"

I gave him an evasive answer, and so he decided to investigate more closely. That night I got my first ride in the back of a police cruiser, and I couldn't help but notice there were no door handles for rear-seat passengers!

Back at police headquarters, the officers managed to get the whole story out of me. They decided I should be their guest in jail until someone responsible came to pick me up. Uncle Virgil and Aunt Sally lived an hour away in Bell Gardens, so they came for me the next morning. After spending a few days at their house, I thanked them for rescuing me and then hitchhiked on to my brother's place.

Don and his wife welcomed me warmly, and I spent the rest of the summer with them. I even started school there in September. But Don's work was changing, and soon he would be moving to a smaller place. I realized there would be no room for me, so I made the difficult phone call to my folks in Oklahoma.

The bus ticket

"Dad? It's Kenneth."

"Yeah? Well, I'd say it's 'bout time we heard from ya."

"It looks like I'm gonna have to come home, Dad, and I was wondering if you could send me the money for a bus ticket."

"Certainly," he said without hesitation, "I'll send you the money."

What a relief! In a few days, I was on my way back to Oklahoma, anxiously wondering how I'd be received, but when I arrived, my folks seemed genuinely glad to have me back!

A little later, I went out to the pasture to see my horse. I called for him, but Blue didn't come. Twenty acres is not a lot of land, but horses can find many places to hide, so I walked clear over to the back end of the pasture, and then I looked through the trees.

Every time I'd ever walked out into the pasture, when Blue saw me, he'd come quickly.

I whistled and called him loudly. "Here, Blue, come here, boy," I called again and again. Usually by this time, he would have come running because I usually had a lump of sugar or some feed for him. But no sound. No Blue. And yet Nellie the mare was there. The cattle were there. But Blue was nowhere to be found.

I checked the fences, and I couldn't figure out why he wasn't there.

I anxiously went back to the house to see if Dad knew what had happened.

"Yep, you rode him home," he said.

His words were like a bolt of lightning. I can still remember how it struck me. I don't remember being mad or becoming hard toward my dad. I just remember that it was like the bottom of my world had fallen out. *Why had I impulsively run away?* I felt more agony for running off and consequently losing my horse than for any other experience while I was growing up. I wanted to blame my dad, but I had caused this situation. I had deserved it. I had done this to myself.

I felt horrible. I'd lost my horse. Blue was the one thing at home that I was connected to. He was my life. There weren't a lot of things that a kid with asthma could do. I couldn't play with the other kids, but I could ride my horse. I could pet him and talk to him. He loved me unconditionally, and now he was gone.

Dad never told me to whom he sold the horse, and I never asked. To this day, I don't know what happened to him, but I never saw Blue again. It took years for the ache in my heart to heal.

After that I became very involved in Future Farmers of America. I remember many times going to a rodeo in town. All the kids would be riding in on their horses, and I'd be walking.

No kids lived nearby; our nearest neighbors lived several miles away. So my dog, Roscoe, was the one I talked to because he was mine. I didn't have a lot of things, but he belonged to me, and he loved me unconditionally.

Roscoe would just sit and watch as I milked the cows, and one day I squirted some milk his way. After that, he'd catch it every time! Dad never caught us. But he did mention that when he milked a cow, he got more milk than I did. "Young man," he'd say, "you're not stripping the cows good."

A couple of years later, when I was in school, I got a letter from Dad. "I just want you to know Roscoe was sitting beside me as I was milking," he said, "and now I know why you never got as much milk as you should have."

Chapter 5

The Amazing Window Shade

A man's enemies are the members of his own household.
—Micah 7:6, NIV

The road to town ran through isolated and sparsely populated country; few visitors, outside of invited folks, ever ventured our way. But the Lord had a plan for our lives, which He put into effect through an interesting set of events.

One day a man stopped by the Morgan house half a mile up the road and left them a magazine called *These Times*. Mrs. Morgan wasn't interested in this religious magazine, so she stuck it in her Sears & Roebuck catalog and promptly forgot about it.

Later that week, Mother needed a Sears & Roebuck catalog, so she went to Mrs. Morgan's house to borrow hers. Back at home, she thumbed through the pages and, discovering the magazine, she began to read. One article in particular caught her interest. It was an article on the seventh-day Sabbath, and it explained that the Scriptures teach that Saturday is the only day God ever set aside as a day of worship. It also said that if a person read only the Bible and nothing else, the only conclusion he or she could possibly draw is that the Lord would have us worship on the day He had sanctified and made holy.

This was a brand-new idea for Mother. She'd never heard of a seventh-day Sabbath, and it quickened her interest because it seemed to make sense. *How will Otto feel about this?* she wondered.

41

Magazine in hand, she walked out to the field where Dad and I were plowing.

"Otto, you need to see this!" she called out, waving the magazine in her hands.

Dad stopped plowing and motioned for me to stop as well. We sat down by the plow as Mother read the article out loud to us.

"Wow! That's a new wrinkle, isn't it?" Dad remarked. "Very interesting. Where did you get the magazine?"

"It was in the Sears catalog I borrowed from Mrs. Morgan," she answered.

"Well then, why don't you take it back and find out where she got it?"

When Mother took the catalog back, she asked Mrs. Morgan about who had given her the magazine.

"I really don't know who he was," she said, "but I'm not interested in it. Go ahead and keep it."

"Well, if he ever comes back, would you have him stop by my house?" Mother asked as she left.

One day a gray-haired, dignified-looking gentleman in his sixties knocked at our door.

"Hello, my name is Henry Morris," he said, "and Mrs. Morgan down the road told me I should stop in here to see you."

Mr. Morris then proceeded to offer us Bible studies, and my parents accepted.

The Sabbath comes into view

From the beginning, the Scriptures captured my interest. I'd never realized the Bible could be so fascinating! For the first time in my life, I could hardly wait to find out more about it each week.

The idea of the seventh-day Sabbath was a totally new revelation to us. The few times I'd attended Sunday School as a child, I'd been taught about the Ten Commandments, but I couldn't help but notice that the fourth commandment read, "Remember the Sabbath day to keep it holy." Now that we were studying the Bible, I decided to ask the pastor about it. When I visited with him, he told me that the Sabbath had been done away with. Innocently, I asked him, "Pastor, *when* was it done away with? Was it recently? Because I remember reading the fourth commandment in Sunday School."

Now, as we began studying the Sabbath, I could see that what the Bible taught was consistent all the way through. In the Old Testament, in Exodus 20:8–11, God clearly placed the seventh-day Sabbath in the Ten Commandments. In Isaiah 58:13, He calls the Sabbath "my holy day"; and in the New Testament, Jesus said in Mark 2:27, 28 that He was the "Lord even of the Sabbath" (NIV).

I realized quickly that keeping the Sabbath was not going to be convenient. In fact, I tried to get around it when Mr. Morris asked me what I was going to do about the Sabbath. "I'll keep every Sunday because it's every seventh day," I told him.

"But the Bible doesn't say a seventh day, it says *the* seventh day," he answered.

I knew he was right, so as we continued to study, it was a new adventure almost every time. I came away with a new understanding of God's Word.

The bear, the beast, and the harlot

Mr. Morris brought out an old pull-down window shade on which he had painted all the beasts of Daniel and Revelation in color! As he rolled it across the living room floor, these strange beasts in Daniel 7 seemed to come to life. There was the lion that represented Babylon; the bear with three ribs in its mouth that depicted Media-Persia; the strange leopard beast with four wings and four heads that stood for the kingdom of Greece. And then there was the fierce dragon with great iron teeth that devoured everything! Mr. Morris explained that it represented pagan Rome. The prophecies of Scripture all of sudden took on meaning. I could see how they fit together perfectly. This increased my faith and helped me understand that the Word of God is true. As the years have passed, I have found these prophecies have been a key to understanding other Bible prophecies too.

It wasn't long before I felt a burning desire to give my heart to the Lord Jesus Christ, and that desire continued to grow. I wanted to walk with Jesus and follow Him! I looked forward to Mr. Morris's visits, and he studied with us for quite some time.

While Dad didn't know much about the Bible, he'd been raised to believe that ministers should not be paid by their parishioners. To his way of thinking, the gospel was free, and preachers should earn their living some other way, taking care of their church business on the side. He'd heard that the apostle Paul had earned his living making tents, and that he'd never received money from the church itself—an erroneous belief, by the way. Although Mr. Morris went around studying and sharing God's Word with people, he was not a minister, and in order to support himself, he would ask the people he studied with to give him their tithe after they had studied together for some time. Unfortunately, when Mr. Morris asked Dad for his tithe, it completely alienated him! In utter disgust, he totally rejected everything he'd learned up to that point.

But Mother and I had seen what the Word of God said. Even though I didn't believe that Mr. Morris was right in asking for tithe, it didn't change what the Bible taught about everything else, so we soon accepted the Bible truths and began to keep the seventh-day Sabbath in our home.

Eventually, a minister from the McAlester Seventh-day Adventist Church got word of our interest and came for a visit. Pastor Winterberg continued studying with Mother and me and helped us get to church. We began to attend regularly, and soon I was baptized—again. My dad's opposition to this was vocal and often accompanied by profanity and violence.

The long road to McAlester

Getting to church each Sabbath became difficult. Each week Mother would ask Dad to take us the two miles into Hartshorne, which he would grudgingly do. There we would catch a streetcar and ride the sixteen miles to McAlester, walking the last stretch to the church. Mother, Dorothy, and I made this trip every Sabbath for years.

Sadly, not much was being done for the children and young people in our church. The congregation knew we were there, but that was about the extent of it. I had grasped the Bible truths and strongly believed them, but there was no real support for our spiritual growth.

"Mother, I think I'll just spend the afternoon in Hartshorne," I would say after church. "It's too hard to keep the Sabbath at home."

She knew that was true, so I'd stay and go to the pool hall for the afternoon, walking the two miles back home at dusk. I did this for quite some time, and all the while Dad's violence increased. Many times I'd come home on Saturday evening to face a beating because I'd gone to church instead of helping him on the farm.

I had loved the time my dad and I had spent together in the outdoors, but after Mother and I began keeping the Sabbath, the only time Dad was willing to go hunting was on Friday night. This nearly broke my heart, since I felt I'd be denying the Sabbath if I went with him. There were many Friday nights when I cried myself to sleep after Dad took off hunting or fishing without me.

Then one day the Lord sent a new couple to our church. Floyd and Mary Roberts took an instant interest in the youth, and that was better than a breath of fresh air during an asthma attack to me! When church was over, they'd invite all the young people to their home, where they would serve us lunch, play Sabbath games, or take walks with us. We'd visit shut-ins, sing, and have long talks too. As I began to understand more of what the Bible taught, I began my walk with the Lord—and I immediately stopped going to the pool hall!

What a blessing Floyd and Mary were to me spiritually. They soon discovered my dad was not supportive, so they offered ideas of things to say and do that might alleviate the situation at home. Some suggestions seemed to work and others didn't, as Dad continued to exhibit anger and bitterness toward Mother and me—and often even toward young Dorothy.

God's red pig

I was going through other struggles too. I was a member of the Future Farmers of America, and one of the requirements was to show an animal at the county fair. With Dad's help, I bought a red pig—a registered Duroc-Jersey sow. I raised her so well that by the time I learned what the Bible taught about clean and unclean meat, my dad and I each had a sow and were well on our way to becoming pig farmers!

As I read what the Bible said in Leviticus 11 and in 2 Corinthians 6 about clean and unclean meats, I came under great conviction that I shouldn't keep my pig. But how would I get rid of her? If Dad even knew what I was thinking, he would probably come close to killing me in anger!

Someone offered to trade me a calf for her, but I wouldn't do that. Another one offered to buy the sow straight out, but I wouldn't do that either. I was young in my understanding of God's Word, and I felt that if it was wrong for me to eat it, it was wrong for anyone else! Of course, today I believe that people need to make their own decision on this matter, in light of what they understand in God's Word.

Finally, in desperation one night, I went into my bedroom, shut the door, and got down on my knees.

"Lord, I don't know what to do with this pig," I prayed. "I can't keep her. I can't sell her, and I can't give her away. So she's no longer my pig. I'm giving her to You! She's Your pig, so please take care of this."

With that, I crawled into bed and enjoyed a peaceful night's sleep. The next morning, I went out on the porch and picked up the slop bucket, but when I got to the pigpen, my pig was laying there dead! Though I loved animals, I had to smile to myself as we dragged the carcass off and buried it. Dad tried his best to find out what caused that sow to die, but he never could figure it out. Of course, I knew the Lord had taken care of my pig problem, and that experience has been a great inspiration to me ever since. God does hear and answer prayers, and He guides with a mighty hand!

Since I wouldn't be showing a pig that year, I decided to show a couple of Southdown sheep instead. They're docile creatures and not very big. But, oh, did they teach me lessons in patience and trust!

As the time for the county fair neared, my agriculture teacher, Mr. Burger, came over to teach me one of the tricks of the trade.

"Here's what we'll do," he began. "A couple of months before the showing, we'll cover the sheep's bodies with gunnysacks, and that will keep their wool nice and clean."

Curious as to how things were going, every few days I'd lift the gunnysacks up and look at their wool. *It's getting dirtier and dirtier! Surely this is not working!* I thought to myself.

Finally, a few days before the fair, Mr. Burger came by the farm again. As we took the gunnysacks off, their wool was almost black! It looked absolutely horrid. Then he took his shears and began cutting off about an inch of nasty-looking wool. As he cut away, I realized that the gunnysacks had somehow pulled all the dirt to the top, revealing their beautiful white wool underneath!

Suddenly, Isaiah 1:18 made perfect sense to me, " 'Come now, let us reason together,' says the LORD. 'Though your sins are like scarlet, they shall be as white as snow; though they are red as crimson, they shall be like wool' " (NIV).

Thinking about church school

Eventually, Mary and Floyd Roberts moved away, and the void was intense. The conviction was growing in my heart that I needed to go away to school to get an education.

"Mother?"

"Yes, Kenneth."

"I've been thinking about my future, and I'd really like to go to school at that place down in Texas the pastor was talking about."

"Why, Kenneth, you know that your dad would never agree for you to go to a church school. Besides, you've never liked school, even when it's free. A school like that would be very expensive. But go ahead and talk to your dad if you want to."

As it turned out, neither one of my parents supported my idea, and Dad, predictably, was strongly opposed. But my conviction was stronger than his objections, so I decided to go anyway. I was seventeen years old and decided that I must do what I believed was right.

Chapter 6

Twenty-two Cents in My Pocket

*Trust in the LORD with all your heart and
lean not on your own understanding.*
—*Proverbs 3:5, NIV*

The Saturday-night beatings from my father and his extreme opposition to my newfound faith had convinced me to leave home and go to school. Pastor Winterberg had invited several of us from his congregation to attend visitors' day at Southwestern Junior College at Keene, Texas. After visiting the campus for a few days, I felt strongly that this was where God was leading me.

Back home, I packed my few belongings in an old suitcase and told my mother where I was going. But I said nothing to Dad because our relationship had hopelessly deteriorated. Then, with twenty-two cents in my pocket, I left home and hitchhiked the 150 miles. I knew no one at the school, and I wasn't even a good student, but I believed the Lord was calling me.

Walking into the registrar's office, I told her I'd come there to go to school but didn't have any money. She promptly sent me to the school's business office, where I repeated my lines.

"I came here to go to school," I announced, "but I don't have any money. I'm willing to work, though, and I need a job."

Perhaps they felt sorry for this scrawny little hundred-pounder who was not quite five feet tall. Out of the kindness of their hearts—and by divine guidance—they let me enroll. I was delighted!

Soon I noticed something else had happened. Something so profound it was impossible to ignore. Once I set foot on that campus, I never again suffered from asthma! It left me then, and has never, ever, returned. What a blessed relief!

To test myself, I even tried out for the tumbling team, just to see if I could do it. Because of my extremely slight build, I was put on the top whenever the troupe did pyramids. *It was like being re-created!* I was able to run and leap, twist and turn, pull and push—and best of all, I could draw in long, wondrously deep breaths of air! I thanked God profusely for my healing.

I was considered a junior in high school, but I had a very sketchy educational background. In fact, I could read only at the third-grade level. Where I came from, what mattered was how well one worked with agriculture and animals, or how one excelled in sports—so I had no idea how incredibly far behind I was compared to my peers. I had to study day and night just to make Cs, and try as I might, I just couldn't seem to grasp what the teachers were talking about. The classes might as well have been taught in a foreign language!

I remember an English class during which our teacher had a student stand up and read a poem by the poet Sidney Lanier, entitled "A Ballad of the Trees and the Master." The first stanza read,

Into the woods my Master went,
Clean forspent, forspent.
Into the woods my Master came,
Forspent with love and shame.
But the olives they were not blind to Him,
The little gray leaves were kind to Him:
The thorn-tree had a mind to Him
When into the woods He came.

"What is that talking about, Kenneth?" the teacher asked.
"I don't have the slightest idea," was my truthful reply.

School was a constant struggle. I studied and worked as much as I possibly could, but regardless of my effort, I fell hopelessly behind in both. My grades were not what I wanted them to be, so I prayed earnestly about them while claiming the promises of God's Word. I studied more and tried harder, and little by little my grades improved, though they were never what I would have liked.

Another strange, but more pleasant phenomenon occurred. Without the asthma, I began to grow, and grow—and grow! Finally caught up in height, but only months into my first school year, I realized how desperately I needed new clothes (long after my classmates noticed, I'm sure). Since everything I earned at school had to go on my school bill, the necessities of life seemed completely out of reach, and I didn't know what to do.

One day I received a note asking me to report to the business office as soon as possible.

"Your school bill is getting quite high," Mr. Bischoff said gravely. "You'll have to do something about it if you're going to remain in school here."

My heart sank. I knew no one else would help with my school bill. I alone was responsible for it.

"Well, I'm working as much as you allow while I'm in school," I replied, "so I guess what you need to do is to increase my salary."

The kind business manager looked over his glasses at the earnest teenager sitting in front of him. He knew my financial situation—and my determination to go to school. I'd tried to be well-behaved, and I was a very hard worker.

"Well, you need to do whatever you can to bring your bill down," he said. "Remember that our school has expenses to meet too."

A faint smile played at the edges of his mouth as he rose and held out his hand to dismiss me.

Now what to do I do? I wondered. *My bill is rising exponentially—no question. But until they tell me I have to leave school, there isn't much I can do except more of what I've been doing—working hard and long.* I began to pray even more.

When my next school bill came, I was in for a big surprise. Much to my amazement, the business manager had indeed given me a significant raise in pay!

About once a semester, the subject came up for discussion again. All I could say was, "I'm working as much as you will allow," and several times I received another raise.

Short pants and cardboard soles

One day a minister and singing evangelist by the name of Charles Keymer came to speak at the school. Although I didn't know him personally, by the providence of God, he singled me out—the youngster whose pants were too short, who had cardboard soles in his shoes. He talked with me for quite a while, and then quietly slipped me a twenty-dollar bill. What a lot of money! I couldn't thank him and God enough. It enabled me to replace my worn-out shoes, get new jeans, a shirt, underclothing, and even toothpaste.

After being in school for nine months, I longed to go back home for a visit, but was afraid I would come down with asthma again. Finally, I did go home and was astonished to discover that God hadn't done a half-baked job! There was no asthma—and it has never bothered me again.

But there were continuing problems at home. Mother and Dad were almost always in a verbal fight, mostly about whether he was being faithful to her or whether she should attend church. Actually, no subject was off-limits in their bitter disagreements. Though my heart ached as I left my sister Dorothy behind in that turmoil, it was a blessing to return to the peace of school.

Although I was a shy kid, the next three years on campus allowed me plenty of time to make friends at my own pace. Though schoolwork came extremely hard and my work was incessant, I enjoyed my experience and came to love and respect the other students and faculty.

Beans in my pocket

Eventually, my bill was so large that I realized I must do something else to earn money. A colporteur program was presented at school, explaining how young men and women could sell religious books door to door for the summer. Some of the students had made enough money canvassing to pay their next year's tuition in full! After listening to the glowing reports from several students, I decided I'd try it for the summer between my junior and senior high-school years. But oddly enough, Mr. Bischoff, the business manager, was neither impressed nor happy about my decision.

"Kenneth," he said, "some kids who try to sell books don't even make enough money to pay their summer living expenses! What you need to do is to stay here and work in the furniture factory, where your income is a sure thing."

But I wouldn't hear of it. I was young, and I really wanted to sell books—so I went without his blessing. I was assigned territory in a town in southern New Mexico, where I worked with another teenager named Don Houghton.

A generous older couple offered us a place in their home rent-free for the summer months while we sold books. Every morning we had worship with Mr. and Mrs. Ives, and this sweet couple prayed for our success every day.

Because we were new at this, Pastor Straley, who was the publishing secretary for the entire Southwestern Union Conference, came down to coach us on how to make book sales. He had considerable experience and now oversaw book sales for all of Arkansas, Louisiana, Oklahoma, Texas, and New Mexico.

"Now boys, I am going to tell you how to earn a scholarship," he said. "The secret to success is to get out there and make presentations, so each morning when you leave the house, I want you to put twenty beans in your left pocket. Then every time you make a presentation, take one bean out of your left pocket and put it in your right pocket. Don't go home until all twenty beans have been moved to your right pocket. If you do that, you'll earn a scholarship!"

"Don," I pleaded, "let me go with you to a house or two and listen to what you say before I go out on my own."

"OK, that's a good idea," he answered.

"I'll tell you what—I'll get us inside the first house, and you make the presentation."

Don agreed, and so I started my canvassing career. We walked up to the first house. I knocked, and a pleasant-looking lady came to the door.

"Good morning, ma'am! I'm Kenneth Cox and this is my friend Don Houghton, and we're from Home Health Education Services, and would like to make a presentation to you."

"Why, thank you, boys. Come on in," she said. "My name is Mrs. Beanblossom."

Her name struck us as hilarious in light of the beans Pastor Straley had suggested we put in our pockets!

Soon it became a real problem for us teenagers because every time Don would say her name during his presentation—which was often—both of us would get so tickled that Don could hardly complete his sentence! He did finally make it through the presentation—and, incredibly, he even made a sale!

Fomentations

Don and I both felt grateful to Mr. and Mrs. Ives for opening their home to us, giving us a place to live that summer. Wanting to do something to show our appreciation, we told Mrs. Ives that when we came in from canvassing in the evening, we'd be glad to help her around the house, wash dishes, and do other chores. Every evening a mountain of dishes was stacked and waiting for us when we came in from selling books. We wondered if she was cleaning out all her cabinets because the stacks were always huge!

At first we didn't think too much of it, but then we began to notice that Mrs. Ives sat in her chair and constantly complained about how badly her legs hurt, as she watched us wash and dry her dishes.

"Mrs. Ives," we said, "we can fix your legs so they won't hurt so much." (We were proud that we'd come up with a bright idea!) "When we come home tomorrow evening, we'll start fomentation treatments on your legs. That should really help them get better."

The next evening we put her feet and lower legs in a large bucket of hot water.

"Mmm," she sighed contentedly, so we left them in the bucket a while. Then we plunged them immediately into a bucket of ice water!

"Oh, they're going to burst! They're going to burst!" she yelled. "Oh! Oh! Oh!"

We were determined to help our landlady, so we continued the leg baptisms back and forth five or six times that evening, and each time the cold water encased her legs, she would scream, "Oh, my legs are going to burst! Oh! Oh! Oh!"

Thinking back on it, we realized that we could have caused her demise—though it was definitely not our intention to harm her. Nevertheless, the next evening when we came in from working there were no dishes to wash—and Mrs. Ives never complained about her legs hurting again!

Taste and see

While canvassing in that town, we met Bill and Marie Hughes and began giving them Bible studies. This was my first experience in taking someone through the Bible truths point by point. It was a thrill to see them reach out in faith and accept the Bible teachings. Because the town had no Seventh-day Adventist church, a little group of us began meeting in a home every Sabbath.

Despite my diligence, after a number of weeks, I'd sold hardly enough books to bother counting! Don, on the other hand, seemed to be doing quite well. As I sank into discouragement, I couldn't help but think that perhaps Mr. Bischoff had been right.

One morning, toward the end of summer, I was so overcome with a feeling of helplessness and discouragement that I fell to my knees. "I simply cannot do this unless You bless me, Lord," I pleaded. "You know how badly I need to make some sales. If I'm doing something wrong, please show me. I want to be a witness for You, so please guide me to those who want to know more about You. And Lord, please impress their hearts to buy the books. Oh, Father, please, help me! Don't even let me go out today without a blessing from You!"

A blessing? Make that plural! God abundantly answered my cry—more than I could ever ask or think! I sold a book or set of books at every house but one in a two-block area. Then, while finishing up my last sale of the day, the lady from the house where I hadn't made a sale came running down the sidewalk.

"I talked my husband into buying the books!" she cried, triumphantly.

During the last two weeks of summer break, I sold enough books to receive a full scholarship—which paid my tuition for the entire school year! I have every reason to believe that God is faithful to those who are faithful to Him.

The next year Don and I decided to go back to the same town and spend another summer canvassing. This time we lived with the Sawyers, who lived in the mountains about fifteen or twenty minutes from town. After spending long days canvassing in the heat, we enjoyed coming back to the mountains in the evenings, where it was cool and pleasant for sleeping. The Lord blessed and guided us, and we both did well and earned scholarships.

An important change came about in my life. Those two summers I spent selling books showed me the joy of leading people to Christ. In fact, I loved it so much that I was fully convicted I should go into the ministry.

"Taste and see that the Lord is good," the Bible says in Psalm 34:8 (NIV).

I had tasted and seen. Nothing would ever satisfy my soul except working to help bring people to Jesus Christ.

Chapter 7

Marriage—and Jail!

A prudent wife is from the LORD.
—Proverbs 19:14, KJV

Back at school I was now a freshman in college. I was actually beginning to enjoy my classes and, with my tuition covered by a hard-earned scholarship, I had more time to get involved in school activities.

It was not really a surprise when I received word that Mother and Dad were divorcing. They were selling the Oklahoma farm and would divide the proceeds. With no other place to go, Mother and Dorothy moved in with Billie, and when I could, I tried to help by sending them some money from my meager earnings.

But life went on, and I couldn't help but notice a certain beautiful young lady on campus. Her name was Marilyn Whitford, and what an amazing, sweet spirit she had! She seemed wise beyond her years,

Kenneth's graduation day at Keene, Texas

and through her soft-spoken and kind demeanor, her genuine love for the Lord was obvious. Marilyn worked as the assistant dean of women, which gave her many opportunities to demonstrate her ability to make sound decisions and remain levelheaded.

Laura Cox and Kenneth

Eventually, I got up enough courage to ask her for a date, and after spending a little time with her, *I was smitten*! We dated for several months, my love for her growing stronger with each passing day. I prayed a lot about our relationship, and when I finally asked her to marry me, I was ecstatic when she consented! I took this as a sign that the Lord was leading and had marvelously answered my prayers.

However, this decision brought a lot of turmoil for Marilyn. People told her that she hadn't used good judgment—considering her future husband's background and his struggle to catch up scholastically.

Her English teacher advised, "Marilyn, I hate to see you make this unwise decision. I'm afraid that Kenneth will never amount to anything and will only drag you down."

Except for the Lord's hand over and under me, I believe her teacher was absolutely right! But God knew how to handle this, and He allowed Marilyn to see beyond the obvious. We completed our sophomore year at Southwestern Junior College, and I was grateful to leave school without owing a penny!

The Green River Ordinance

We decided to marry in June 1955 in Oklahoma City, where Marilyn's family lived. It was a simple wedding—sweet and beautiful. For our honeymoon we went directly to Hobbs, New Mexico, where we rented a two-room furnished apartment, and I began selling books again. How happy we were to be serving the Lord—together!

Kenneth and Marilyn cutting wedding cake

Since we wanted to save money toward finishing our last two years in college, we decided not to attend school in the fall, but to work and put money aside instead. When Marilyn was offered a teaching position in El Paso, Texas, at the end of the summer, we packed our car with everything we owned and moved. The Lord blessed, and we enjoyed that special time in our lives.

Las Cruces, New Mexico, was only thirty-five miles from El Paso, and one day I felt impressed to canvass that area too. So a young man named Johnny Cox (no relation) and I began working that city. Things went well and we sold many books—until one day we ran afoul of the law!

I had just come from making a sale in a large home when I saw Johnny standing beside a police car down the street. I hurried down to see what the problem was. Coming up behind the two, I asked breathlessly, "Is anything wrong?"

I apparently startled the officer because he arrested us both on the spot, citing a Green River Ordinance and stating that we needed a license to sell. That day I got to enjoy my second ride in a patrol car!

We were thrown in jail with hardly any opportunity to defend ourselves, though we were allowed one phone call. I frantically called Victor Rice, the publishing secretary for the local church conference office.

"Pastor Rice? This is Kenneth Cox, and Johnny Cox is here with me. Listen, we're in some pretty big trouble. We felt impressed to come over to Las Cruces and sell books here, but a few minutes ago we were arrested, and now they're putting us in jail. They say we have to pay a big fine or stay in jail. Is there anything you can do to help us? This is the only phone call they're allowing!"

"Oh, Kenneth, I'm so sorry to hear that," he answered. "Listen, I'll leave here immediately for Las Cruces to see what I can do, but remember that there are three hundred miles between us! It's going to take a while for me to drive that far, but I'll be praying for you all the way. You pray for my safety also."

Soon we discovered that most of the inmates with us were in there for serious and violent crimes, such as murder, rape, and bank robberies. Some were even waiting to be transported to Leavenworth Prison to serve out their sentences. Johnny and I felt like Paul and Silas in that cell. Night was coming on, and we breathed a prayer asking the Lord for His protection—and for His protection over Pastor Rice.

We both sat on the bed in that filthy jail cell—we dared not lie down. The smell made us nauseated, and the inmates looked threatening as they eyed us curiously. I'm sure we were quite a sight.

"Where ya from?" one of them asked.

"Whadja do?"

"Why're ya in jail?"

"Who's your lawyer?" It seemed like everyone had questions.

When they heard that Johnny and I were there for selling religious books, the inmates became very angry. They shouted for the guard and rattled the cell door.

This was not what we expected, and Johnny and I exchanged nervous glances as we prayed for protection. The inmates cursed the guard unmercifully.

"What's this world coming to—putting these guys in jail for selling religious books?"

As things quieted down, one of the rough-looking men turned to me and asked, "So whadda ya believe?"

"You know," I began, "it doesn't matter much what I believe. What matters for eternity is what the Bible teaches."

I prayed a silent prayer for God to speak through me, since the last thing I was prepared for was to give these inmates a Bible study.

"The Bible teaches that God loves us all—so much that He was willing to allow His Son to come to this earth and die for us just to prove it." I glanced over our cell companions. Without a doubt, some of them were murderers and bank robbers, but they were listening intently. "God longs for us to come to Him, confess our sins, and allow Him to change us."

I quoted John 3:16 and 17: "For God so loved the world, that he gave his only begotten Son, that whosoever believeth in him should not perish, but have everlasting life. For God sent not his Son into the world to condemn the world; but that the world through him might be saved" (KJV).

Then I quoted 1 John 1:9: "If we confess our sins, he is faithful and just to forgive us our sins, and to cleanse us from all unrighteousness" (KJV).

For several hours, Johnny and I shared our faith in Christ and in what He is willing to do for each person who accepts Him. We both shared our personal testimony too. Occasionally, one of the men would interrupt with a question, but it was obvious there was little disbelief among them as they soaked up every drop of truth. They seemed to be searching for meaning in their lives and were very much aware of their need for change.

"You know, fellas," I said, "God loves each of you just as much as He loves Johnny and me. In fact, He allowed His Son to leave the splendors of heaven to come to this dark world to live, suffer, and die, so you could be saved. He longs to give you forgiveness and peace, and maybe, just maybe, God had a plan in putting us here with you to-night. Tell you what—I'm going to pray a prayer for each of us, and if it's your desire to ask Jesus to forgive your sins and live in your heart from this day forward, just say 'Amen' when I'm done praying."

I began praying, pleading with God for their hearts. Several runny noses developed around the room, and when the prayer ended, the sound of "Amen" seemed to come from every part of that cell. Soon afterward, several of them drifted off into a peaceful sleep, while others continued asking questions.

Pastor Rice finally arrived at about 3:00 A.M. and paid our fines. Since "all things work together for good," I have often wondered if God might have used our testimony that night to turn any of the prisoners around. I look forward to finding out in heaven. As we walked out of jail, Pastor Rice told us to forget Las Cruces and return to El Paso *pronto,* and continue selling there.

I'll take you to court!

One day my phone rang. It was a lady we'd met in Las Cruces. "I heard you boys were put in jail for selling books," she said, "but some fellows just came by my house selling religious books today! I called the courthouse and asked why they hadn't picked them up and put *them* in jail, and they answered, 'We don't put people in jail for selling books.' I repeated my question, and they never would give me a straight answer!"

Johnny and I decided to go back to Las Cruces and check it out.

"Could we purchase a license to sell books here?" I asked at city hall.

"Sorry, but you can't buy a license," the clerk replied. "There's a Green River Ordinance here, and you can't sell religious books in this city."

"Well, we heard that some other people are selling books, and they don't seem to have a problem," we responded.

"We're sorry, but we're not giving you a license to sell books here. You can't work here." The clerk was not backing down, and there was something strange about the answer we kept getting.

Johnny and I made what we thought was a very convincing case. In fact, we tried everything we could think of, but we didn't get anywhere. As we drove out of town, I had a bright idea.

"Let's go see the editor of the newspaper. Maybe he can help us."

The newspaper editor was a large, rather rough-looking character. He sat behind his big cluttered desk and listened to us explain our situation and our prior arrest. I noticed he became visibly upset as the story unfolded. Soon he picked up the phone and called city hall.

"Listen to me! I'm sending these two young men back down there, and you need to give them a license to sell books!" he yelled. "If you don't, I'm taking you to court, and you know I will because I've done it before! You give them a license, and I mean *now*!"

He slammed down the receiver. "Well, I guess that's about all I can do for you here," he said, laughing. "Go back to city hall and see if they won't give you a license now."

We thanked the editor for his help and made our way back to city hall. Again we approached the clerk. "We were told we could get a license here to sell books door-to-door," we said as politely as we could.

"Just wait a minute. I'll check on that," she replied.

That "minute" turned into two or three hours while we sat waiting patiently. After it became obvious that we were not going to leave, the clerk finally called us back to the counter.

"That will be fifteen dollars," she said, pushing our licenses toward us.

We immediately went out and started canvassing the area.

"Oh, you're those boys selling books," we heard several times from those who came to the door. "The priest told us to just slam the door in your faces if you came by."

Thankfully, curiosity overcame many of the housewives. The Lord blessed, and we sold many books.

The year past very quickly and soon we were headed to Union College, a Seventh-day Adventist school in Lincoln, Nebraska.

Chapter 8

The Strange Case of the S&H Green Stamps

"Fear not, for I am with you; be not dismayed, for I am your God."
—Isaiah 41:10a, NKJV

Life in Lincoln was very different from what Marilyn and I were used to in the Southwest. The campus was beautiful and lush, and the students and teachers were a blessing. We rented an apartment from Mrs. Eno, who lived directly across from the boys' dorm. It was really a converted attic—two rooms on the third floor. At the top of the stairs, our front door opened into a small living room, and the bedroom and kitchen were combined. Because the ceiling sloped rather drastically in that room, we shoved our bed under the low end in order to maximize the size of the room—making sure we remembered not to sit up when we got out of bed, or we would bump our heads! Though tiny, the apartment was comfortable, and we enjoyed making our home there. I painted houses to help provide an income while Marilyn worked at the dry cleaners around the corner. And, of course, we had scholarships from selling books to cover our tuition.

Our first baby was due to make an appearance, and I had been in bed with the flu for two days when Marilyn said, "Kenneth, I think it's time to go to the hospital!"

Still quite sick, I got out of bed and drove her to the hospital, where our first child was born. We named her Laura Ruth after my mother, and our precious little girl became the delight of our eyes and hearts. Marilyn quit school and stayed home to care for her, and we both eagerly looked forward to my graduation from Union College, after which I planned to attend the Seventh-day Adventist Seminary in Washington, D.C. During our stay at Union, we wanted to do something to help advance God's work and bless others, so we began driving fifty miles each way to a little church in York, Nebraska, where I preached. I still marvel at the kindness and patience of those dear people who let me "practice" on them. Bless their hearts, they even encouraged me.

This was so different from what I had experienced in El Paso, Texas. My dear folks there had whispered to Marilyn, "I'm afraid Kenneth just doesn't have what it takes to make it as a minister." Or, "Marilyn, his grammar is really bad." Or, "I don't know how he was able to get through school; he just seems so uneducated and uncultured." When I spoke, colloquialisms often popped out (as they do even now), and some folks laughed inappropriately, keeping my self-confidence low. But God's promise in 2 Corinthians 12:9 has always been one of my favorites: "My strength is made perfect in weakness" (KJV). After marrying Marilyn, my grades went from Cs to As! All the credit goes to the Lord, of course, and to my wife—they both helped me to understand my studies and to grow intellectually.

Seminary days

Graduation day from Union College finally came, and what a time of rejoicing it was! Then, off we went to the Seventh-day Adventist Theological Seminary in Washington, D.C. We had already received an invitation from the Texico Conference (a conference that included eighty-six counties in Texas and all of New Mexico) to come work as a pastor somewhere when I graduated. With this future commitment, the Texico Conference would now sponsor me at the seminary. That meant that I could focus on my studies as Marilyn worked to cover our living expenses.

What a blessing that was! I was now able to spend hours and hours, studying and learning. I soaked up every gem possible from the excellent teachers who were rich in knowledge of Bible prophecy, Greek, Hebrew, archaeology, biblical interpretation, New Testament, Old Testament—you name it! And because the seminary building was right beside the General Conference headquarters, many times we would have guest speakers from various parts of the world. These men had worked on the front lines of missions and had lifetimes of experience in taking the gospel to the entire world.

Rheumatic fever

The seminary assigned all of us student pastors to churches, and Marilyn and I were assigned to the church at Annapolis, Maryland. At Christmastime, our church decided to go caroling, so each night we sang door-to-door, collecting donations for the needy. One night it was colder than usual, and by the next day, Marilyn had developed quite a sore throat. It grew steadily worse, so I took her to the doctor. After examining her and looking at the results of her throat culture, Doctor Weatherton said, "Mrs. Cox, your throat is very inflamed, and our lab work shows that you have strep throat. Here's a prescription that should get you back on your feet in four or five days. Be sure to take it twice a day until it's all gone."

Marilyn began taking the medicine that night, but after the second dose, she felt even worse. Nauseated, she could hardly think of eating, and by the next day, she was vomiting.

"Kenneth, would you call Mrs. Morris and see if she could watch Laura until you get home tonight?" she asked. "I feel ill."

"I wonder if it's the flu," I said, to which she responded, "I don't know, but whatever it is, it's not fun!"

The next day Marilyn could hardly get out of bed. Her head hurt, and the nausea and vomiting continued. I took her back to the doctor, and this time he found that not only was she dehydrated, but she was also suffering from rheumatic fever, which she had contracted several times as a child. It had not resurfaced for many years. Marilyn needed to be hospitalized immediately, where she would remain for several weeks on complete bed rest until her heart could recover.

This was shocking news! Not only was my dear wife gravely ill, but she was also our only breadwinner! Once I was sure Marilyn was as comfortable as possible, I went back to our apartment to arrange for our daughter's care.

I called Marilyn's mother. "Of course," she said over the phone, "we'll drive up from Oklahoma to Washington and get that precious little bundle immediately. And don't you worry; we'll keep her as long as necessary. Let that be the least of your worries, Kenneth. We'll do whatever we can to help."

I knew she meant it, and how grateful I was for godly in-laws! Feeling my need, I fell on my knees and poured my heart out to God. *Lord, we need a miracle right now. Marilyn is so sick, but You are the Great Physician. Please, please heal her. I can't stand to see her suffer. And You know that we're trying to prepare to work for You. Marilyn wants to be part of that. Our baby needs her mother. You also know that we need Marilyn's salary for it to happen—otherwise, how are we going to pay for our rent and food and utilities and gasoline, and all the other things we need? Please, please heal her—if it is Your will. But help me know what to do. You know that we both want to serve You. Thank You for whatever Your answer is.*

Learning to trust

I began to take inventory. I had made enough money selling books so that with the sponsorship, my education was covered. But no matter how I figured things, there simply was not enough money to feed and shelter my family and send money for our daughter's care—not to mention a large hospital bill that would be coming all too soon.

That evening, I went back to Marilyn's hospital room and sat down on the bed beside her.

"Honey," I said, "I think I need to quit school and go to work until you're better. Once you are well, I'll finish up at the seminary."

She looked at me incredulously. With love in her voice, she asked softly, "Kenneth, why don't we trust God for what He says?"

"I . . . I don't understand what you mean."

"Well," she replied, "we've been faithful in serving the Lord. We've returned our tithe and dedicated our lives to Him. Let's step out in faith. I think you should continue going to school, and we'll see what the Lord will do."

The whole idea was really hard for me because I'd worked my way through school and had been responsible for my expenses. Now the idea of stepping out in faith, depending totally on the Lord to get us through, was a giant step for me! I hadn't completely learned the lesson of faith yet.

Within three days, Marilyn's parents had picked up Laura, and that responsibility had been resolved, albeit with many tears. We decided to sell our car, and I would walk the three miles to the seminary; but because the car wasn't worth much, the money from its sale didn't last long. Marilyn was still in the hospital. *What in the world will we do?* I wondered. Falling to my knees, again I prayed earnestly that God would somehow work in our behalf. We had done everything we knew to do—except I hadn't quit school.

Then a series of miracles began to unfold. God in His kindness, mercy, and love opened the windows of heaven through His saints on earth. One day I found what appeared to be an empty envelope in our mailbox. But when I looked in it, I found twenty dollars!

Praise God! I thought. Then in the next few days, another "letter" appeared—and then another and another. The slender envelopes would contain twenty, twenty-five, or even thirty dollars! Other times, a fat envelope full of S&H Green Stamps would appear in my mailbox. These extremely popular stamps were easily traded for cash or household products from their catalog or stores. At one point, the Green Stamps catalog was the largest publication in the United States, and the company issued three times as many Green Stamps as the United States Postal Service issued postage stamps!

This went on day after day, week after week. The letters were not from just one place, but from all over the United States. Usually they had no return address—just a postmark to give me some idea of where they had come from. Finally, the joyous day arrived when Marilyn had recovered enough for baby Laura to return to us.

Miraculously, God took care of our needs in every way because I finished the seminary without owing the school, the doctors, or the hospital a single penny! Oh how good God is, and how wonderfully His hand provides! Isn't it just like Him?

I think of Christ asking His disciples, "Did you lack anything?" And they said, "Nothing" (see Luke 22:35). Marilyn and I could say we had not lacked a single thing, either. The years at the seminary were a wonderful time of growth, both in faith and in understanding God's Word, but now we were anxious to know where our first assignment would be, and we were eager to get to work!

Chapter 9

H. M. S. Jr.

*"I will strengthen you and help you; I will uphold you
with my righteous right hand."*

—Isaiah 41:10b, NIV

Soon Marilyn and I were on our way to Albuquerque, and we could hardly believe that I was to intern under Pastor H. M. S. Richards Jr. (He was named after his father, the famous speaker for the international *Voice of Prophecy* radio broadcast, and his initials stood for Harold Marshall Sylvester.) Harold was a big man physically, and had an infectious wit and personality. He never seemed to meet a stranger, and everywhere he went, people knew and loved him.

I stood in awe of this man who seemed larger than life. Harold had been raised in the Seventh-day Adventist Church, so he knew the organization and operations all the way to the top—even calling the men at the world headquarters by name. It was generally known that he was his father's heir apparent, and I felt certain that he had no idea of what he was getting when this very green, new pastor was assigned to work with him.

Marilyn and I rented an unfurnished apartment and bought a mattress, which we put on the floor. Our kitchen table was a box, but we were thrilled to be starting work in this wonderful district of Albuquerque. It was soon time to go out visiting church members with Pastor Richards, and when lunchtime came that first day, he said, "Let's go have lunch at Bob and Jeanette's home."

He knocked on the door, and when Jeanette answered, he announced, "Hi! We've come to have lunch with you!" Amazingly, the family seemed happy to feed the two hungry ministers, and even acted very pleased that their pastors had stopped by and invited themselves to lunch! As a matter of fact, because of his magnetic personality, I don't remember ever going home to eat while we were out visiting. We always went to the closest church member's home and invited ourselves in!

The soloist

Pastor Richards decided to hold an evangelistic meeting in Grants, a town seventy miles away, which was booming because of the nearby uranium mines. This was a new experience for me all around, since I had no experience in putting up a large tent or caring for it.

We found a vacant lot, and with the help of several church members, we pitched the tent, built a platform, and set up all the chairs. We were almost ready for opening night when Pastor Richards dropped a bomb!

"Kenneth," he said, "you'll need to lead the music each evening."

Uh-oh! Music and I didn't even dwell together on the same planet! There was probably no minister on earth more musically illiterate than I was—nor one more musically astute than H. M. S. Jr.

I painfully recalled how inadequate I felt when I had been required to take a conducting class as part of my theology requirements. During our second class the teacher had asked, "Does anyone here play piano?"

A girl raised her hand, and the teacher asked her to play a certain hymn.

"Now, can anyone tell me what time signature or meter that song was written in?" She might just as well have asked what time it was on the moon! I knew there was such a thing, but I hadn't the foggiest idea how to tell if it was 3/4 or 4/4 meter just by listening. (I still don't!)

I passed the class only by the generous mercy of my teacher. But now it seemed there was no way out! *Maybe, by the grace of God, I can fake it,* I thought.

A few days later, though, Pastor Richards dropped another bomb by telling me I needed to sing a solo too!

"A solo?" I sputtered. "A solo? Man, you have to be crazy! I can't even carry a tune!"

Pastor Richards stood up to his full six feet, four inches. "Well, you'll need to sing a solo every night, so start practicing!" he said with only the slightest twinkle in his eye.

To say I was frightened is the understatement of the century! On opening night, my knees were shaking, and my voice quivered first here, and then there, throughout the hymn. Every time I got off-key, I would hear him behind me, singing the right notes to get me back on track! Even now I shudder with embarrassment at the thought of the "special music" those people "enjoyed."

But for the grace of God

One evening after the meeting, he said, "Kenneth, I'm going back to Albuquerque to take care of some business. Would you look after the tent while I'm gone? I'll be back tomorrow afternoon in plenty of time for the meeting."

That night a huge storm came up, and the wind began to howl. I jumped into the car and raced down to the tent as fast as I could, but already the sides were billowing like a gigantic balloon. I grabbed the ropes, trying to hold the tent down, but the wind picked me up off the ground and slung me around as if I were a grasshopper. Hanging on for dear life, I prayed, but then, all of a sudden, a great gust of wind picked up the entire tent and shook it! The side poles began to snap like toothpicks, the tent heaved a long, eerie sigh, and then it collapsed gracefully and quietly to the ground. The next morning I surveyed the damage and tried to put things back together. Fortunately, the center poles had not fallen, but almost all the side poles were broken, so I went to the lumber yard and bought some eight-foot-long two-by-fours. By driving a large spike into one end, I was able to make these boards work as side poles. Everything was back in place in time for the meeting that evening, and the evangelistic series continued.

A few days later, I was preparing the tent for the evening meeting when a car pulled up, and five dirty, unshaven fellows piled out. They looked like a bunch of thugs! Then suddenly I recognized them as the guys I'd grown up with! The coal mines in Oklahoma had closed down, and they'd come to Grants to work in the uranium mines.

Now every one of them was either an alcoholic or a drug addict, and my mind began to race as I looked at them. *Dear God, had it not been for Your mercy and goodness, this could have been me!*

My friends greeted me warmly and said they'd like to get some coffee. Because there was a restaurant across the street, I went with them so we could visit. Meanwhile, Pastor Richards drove up and found no one at the tent. He knew I couldn't be far away, since my car was there, so he walked into the restaurant and spotted me sitting at a table with my rough-looking friends. He motioned me over.

"Who are those panhandlers?" he whispered.

"These are guys I grew up with, Harold. Would you like to meet them?"

Of course, he graciously invited my friends to the meeting, but I had the feeling that he had a hard time relating to my rough-mannered friends. For me, though, this experience was an overwhelming reminder that God's merciful hand had definitely been over my life.

Our time interning in Albuquerque under Pastor Richards was short lived. Marilyn and I were called to pastor a district of three churches: Dalhart, Texas, where we lived; Clayton, New Mexico (39 miles away); and Raton, New Mexico (121 miles away)!

Chapter 10

Why, Dear God?

"My grace is sufficient for you, for My strength is made perfect in weakness."
—*2 Corinthians 12:9, NKJV*

I had no idea how severe the weather could be in the Texas Panhandle. The wind blew constantly all year, except during August. The wind was so strong that at every funeral service, as soon as a grieving family walked out of church, all the flowers were snatched away and shredded by the wind. In winter, the cattle stood with their backs to the wind; otherwise, the wind would blow snow up their nostrils and suffocate them! Often, the fences would be covered over with snow—even when there was no snow on the ground. It was almost always piled high around the houses too. Snowdrifts were expected on roads long after it quit snowing, and although snowplows would come through, the wind would shriek and dance and, within a few hours, pile the snow again into huge, unpredictable drifts.

I would have had to visit my churches less regularly had I not discovered a unique feature about my Volkswagen Bug. You see, the steel sheet that effectively sealed off the underside of the car acted like a sled. If I hit a snowdrift at good speed, I could slide right through to the other side!

Even so, the highway patrol often refused to let me travel the eighty-two miles of open range when the winds were extreme. One time I was headed to Raton when the police closed the road. As I retraced my way, I was startled to see the local Catholic priest, an elderly man, standing out in the middle of the road. The wind was blowing so hard he couldn't move. I stopped my car and was able to help him get back into the rectory. It wasn't safe to be out, even in a vehicle, during a violent windstorm. Along with the wind, the temperatures were often extremely low—the frigid air seemingly blowing in straight from the North Pole. But in spite of these harsh physical elements, Marilyn and I learned to love this area and its warmhearted people.

Kenneth preaching

The drive from our home in Dalhart, Texas, to Clayton, New Mexico, was only thirty-nine miles, but because we crossed over into a different time zone, we gained an hour. This made it possible for me to preach in Dalhart at 9:30 A.M. and then drive to Clayton for the 11:00 A.M. service. Then after a quick lunch, our family could make it in time for an afternoon service in Raton, another eighty-two miles away.

For five years we essentially spent every Sabbath in our tiny Volkswagen, but thanks to Marilyn's ingenuity and good humor, we played Bible games, sang songs, colored, and had picnics—making what could have been very long days into happy and fun family times.

The great northerner

I invited Cyril Miller, stewardship secretary for the Southwestern Union of Seventh-day Adventists, to hold evangelist meetings in

Dalhart. We found a vacant lot in a prominent place that seemed just right for the meeting, but this time we rented an air tent, which I had never used before. The inflatable tent, similar to a very thick balloon, even came with carpeting. One advantage was that it could be heated—a necessity with the cold weather coming.

Our church members worked hard at making everything appealing. They even built a platform with a large, attractive backdrop that rose up behind the pulpit to within a foot of the tent's roof. The meetings began with a good attendance—but then it began to snow!

At first it didn't seem to be a big problem because the tent was heated. As the snow fell, it would slide down the sides and pile up until it was about two feet deep around the edges. This actually helped insulate the tent, making it very comfortable inside. Everything went well until one night during the meeting, a northerner blew in. The winds howled fiercely, and the snow blew sideways. The gusts hit the tent like a gigantic boxing glove, caving in the sides and then popping them back out. It was more than frightening!

What no one had noticed was that the snow around the tent had been melting from the heat inside. And, of course, the ground holding the tent stakes had also been softening. Now each time the wind hit the tent, the stakes loosened a bit more.

Then it happened! The wind doubled up both fists and hit the tent soundly. One side tore into the corner of the backdrop, punching a gaping hole in the roof. Immediately, the wind whipped through the tent, and with one mighty gust, ripped it from one side to the other!

Pastor Miller found himself standing alone on the platform—in the open air—with the entire congregation underneath the tent before him!

It happened so fast that no one panicked, and with many helpful volunteers, everyone got out without injury. But it did deal a fatal blow to our meetings. In spite of the fact that we tried moving to the church, the intense storm continued relentlessly until we finally canceled the meetings.

Kenneth Randall

Marilyn and I didn't want to raise Laura as an only child, but after Marilyn's bout with rheumatic fever, we felt it best to consult with a physician before planning for more children. After giving Marilyn a thorough examination, Dr. Blackstone said he thought she was healthy enough to have another child without any significant problem. We hoped for a boy to round out our family.

"Of course," he reminded us, "you should seek early prenatal care and keep a close watch for any abnormalities."

Marilyn's pregnancy went smoothly until the fifth month, when she began having trouble breathing. Her doctor said her heart was not able to handle the additional load and that she must have complete rest. But with a little girl to care for, along with the demands of being a minister's wife, Marilyn simply couldn't get the rest she needed at home.

After talking it over, we concluded it would be best if she stayed with her parents until the baby came. My in-laws were delighted at the prospect, and Marilyn rested and thoroughly enjoyed the time with her parents.

Oklahoma City is three hundred miles from Dalhart, so I was able to visit during breaks. Everything went well until the seventh month, when Marilyn began having trouble breathing again. Her parents took her to see Dr. Cathey, a cardiologist, who put her in the hospital immediately and said she must stay there on complete bed rest until the baby arrived.

The pregnancy was tricky for the next two months. Marilyn's doctors decided that she should give birth naturally, without a Cesarean section, because of her heart condition. But the birth was premature, and Kenneth Randall lived only fifteen hours. He was a beautiful baby in every way, but his lungs would not expand and he could not breathe. What we had hoped for and desired was gone. Marilyn wanted so badly to have this baby to make our family complete. *Why dear God? Why?* we asked. There just didn't seem to be an answer.

With the death of our child, part of me died too.

Death is so final. I couldn't change things. We had prayed and asked the Lord to intervene, hoping the baby would live. But now I faced the reality that even though I was thankful that Marilyn had lived through the pregnancy, our hopes for another child had evaporated.

The funeral service was just a simple graveside committal. How lonely I felt—my wife lying in the hospital, even as I laid my infant son to rest.

How I long for the day when Christ will return, and families will be reunited again. But on this old earth, death is so final. My son was resting in Jesus, but I had another crisis before me, which left me without time to grieve my loss at that time.

A miracle

After that tragic experience, Marilyn's health began to deteriorate rapidly. I came into her hospital room the next morning but could not awaken her. I called the nurse and asked, "Do you know what's wrong with my wife? I can't wake her."

Without answering, she immediately called the doctor over the intercom. In a matter of moments, the cardiologist was examining her.

"Mr. Cox," he said, "I'm sorry to tell you, but your wife is dying. She is suffering from mitral stenosis caused by the rheumatic fever she has had earlier. The mitral valve of her heart is closing, and is not letting enough blood through."

Two other doctors came in and began discussing her case. One was a heart surgeon by the name of Dr. Manuel.

"Doctor, is there any hope?" I pleaded. "Would surgery help?"

"No, she would just die sooner," was his stark response. He abruptly turned and left the room.

I felt myself reeling. *Dear God, help us!* was all I could think to pray. I touched Marilyn's cold hand. *Lord, please spare her life so we can be a family and raise our little girl together.*

A few minutes later, Dr. Manuel walked back into the room and said, "Mr. Cox, if you're willing to take the chance, I will operate." Why he changed his mind, I didn't know. Perhaps God impressed him. *This could be God opening a door!* And by faith I decided we should walk through it.

"Go ahead," I said. "The sooner, the better."

The hospital staff went into action immediately. Marilyn's blood pressure had dropped dangerously low, so when they tried to start an IV, they discovered that her veins had collapsed. Now they had to perform a venous cutdown in order to insert the needle.

Five hours later, they rolled Marilyn out of the operating room. Her blood pressure was normal, her heartbeat was normal, and the mitral valve was working as it should. When the surgeon came out, I asked, "What happened?"

Dr. Manuel looked me straight in the eye and said, "What took place here today was a miracle." Then, without any further explanation, he again turned and left.

The Lord in His goodness and mercy had given me back my beloved wife! But my rejoicing was short lived. Now that her heart was operating as it should, the fluid that had built up in her tissues began to be rapidly excreted by her kidneys. While this was a good thing, it also caused a drastic drop in her electrolytes. This nightmarish roller coaster continued for days. One day she wouldn't have enough potassium, and the next day she had too much.

One morning I came to see her and, once again, I could not awaken her even though she seemed to be breathing normally. This time I ran to the nursing station and said, "Something is wrong with my wife! I can't wake her up!"

The nurse didn't seem nearly as concerned as I was. "Mr. Cox," she said calmly, "your wife is in a coma. A doctor will be in to see you shortly to explain what's happening. This is not unusual when someone has been as ill as she has. Why don't you just wait in your wife's room until he gets there?"

After what seemed an eternity, a psychiatrist came in and explained that the coma was caused by the near-death ordeal she had gone through. I didn't understand much of what he said until I heard the words, "She should come out of the coma in a few days. I'd suggest you talk to her and let her know that you're here. Even though she doesn't appear to respond, it will help her through this period."

For several days, I talked to Marilyn and read books to her as she lay there—not uttering a single word or sound. Then one day, as I was standing beside her bed, talking, she opened her eyes.

"Kenneth! How long have I been asleep?" she asked. In her mind it had only been a few hours.

From that point on, she improved each day, and before long she was out of the hospital. How we praised the Lord!

Another answer to prayer

We had so hoped to have another child, but now that hope was gone. However, about a year later, Marilyn brought up a new idea.

"What do you think about adopting a child?" she asked.

"Well, I don't know," I replied. "I've never given it much thought. Why don't we make it a matter of prayer? If this is what the Lord wants, I'm sure He will open up a way. I don't think there would be any difference in how we felt toward the child," I continued, "because you certainly can't love a child until you have one. So what difference does it make if we adopt?"

We both realized we had no idea how to adopt, but a woman's innate desire for a child always finds a way, and before long Marilyn was corresponding with an agency in another state. After supplying all the background information and waiting several months, we received a phone call.

"A young woman will soon be giving birth but is unable to keep her baby. Are you interested?"

"Yes, of course, we are interested! Yes! Yes! A boy or girl—it doesn't matter."

Although we received very little information, we were thrilled at the prospect. We just hoped the baby would be healthy.

Marilyn was delighted and passed on her excitement to little Laura. I was happy that they were happy, though I admitted I had only thumbs and no fingers when it came to dealing with babies!

A couple of weeks later, the phone rang again.

"We have a sweet little boy, two days old," the nurse said. "He's waiting for you to come and bring him home!"

In a couple of hours, Marilyn, Laura, and I were driving to San Bernardino, California, a thousand miles away. We drove straight through, anxious to get there. Marilyn and the agency had done such a good job with the paperwork, that in a matter of minutes after arrival we were holding our precious little boy in our arms. James Russell was truly a bundle of joy—bright-eyed, beautiful, and alert. We both knew that he was God's special gift to us.

We called him Jim, or Jimmy, and now that our family was complete, no parents could ever have been more proud of their children. They were both precious gifts from our loving God.

Chapter 11

The Smoking Deacon

Whenever I am afraid, I will trust in You.
—Psalm 56:3, NKJV

The congregation in Clayton had decided to build a new church, which they greatly needed. So our family moved there because most of the building would have to be done by church members, and I would need to supervise. Although I didn't realize it, the Lord knew that when it came to ministry, I had some growing to do.

My head deacon was Dewey, a very mild-mannered man who operated a welding shop and was loved by all. One day I stopped by and spotted him in the corner, welding, his helmet pulled part way down over his face. But there was something odd going on. *He was smoking a cigarette!*

I couldn't believe my eyes. My head deacon was *smoking*!

Totally dumbfounded, I turned and walked out of his shop before he saw me. As his pastor, I was embarrassed and shocked. *How shall I handle this?* I hadn't had a class at the seminary on what to do in such cases, but I didn't want to discourage my friend and brother. *What can I say or do to help?*

I labored and prayed over this issue for several months, returning three times to his welding shop. Each time, Dewey was welding with a cigarette in his mouth, but he never knew his pastor had been there.

Finally, I decided I had to do something because I just couldn't keep going in and looking! I went to his shop one more time. Sure enough, there was Dewey, welding away with a cigarette in his mouth. I walked up behind him.

"How are you doing, Dewey?" I said with a loud voice.

Quicker than lightning, he reached up and grabbed his lit cigarette out of his mouth, stuffing it in his pocket!

"Dewey," I laughed, "get that cigarette out of your pocket! You'll catch your pants on fire!"

He pulled out the cigarette and threw it to the floor. His hand was burned, but that was the least of his concerns. He hung his head, shame written all over his face.

"Do you really want to smoke, Dewey?" I asked.

"No, Pastor," he replied. "It's the plague of my life, but I just can't seem to quit."

"Well, Dewey, if you really want to quit, I'll tell you what I'll do. I'll come here to your shop every day, and we'll kneel down and pray about it until the Lord gives you victory."

As we prayed that day, we both felt a tremendous relief, and it wasn't long before Dewey no longer smoked. His desire for cigarettes was completely taken away!

That day I learned that my responsibility is never to condemn, but to help. As Jesus put it, "God did not send his Son into the world to condemn the world, but to save the world through him" (John 3:17, NIV).

Throw yourself before the Lord

Now that I had my own district, I was eager to hold evangelistic meetings. It had been my passion to introduce men and women to Jesus Christ since I'd learned of Him, so along with my pastoral responsibilities, I held public meetings in both Dalhart and Clayton— with little to no response.

I prayed long and hard, pleading with the Lord to give the small churches more souls for His kingdom, but my prayers seemed to go almost unanswered. Why weren't we seeing more results? If this is what the Lord wanted me to do, where was the blessing? Should I just forget about evangelism and devote all my time to pastoring my churches?

Marilyn supported me in whatever I wanted to do. It was never a question about staying in ministry. It was simply a matter of working at it and not seeing any results. I was really in a quandary, not knowing which way to turn.

What happened next was a pivotal point in my life. I heard of the meetings Pastor E. E. Cleveland was conducting in Southern California, so I decided to take some vacation time and drive out to attend them. Perhaps I could get an idea of what I was doing wrong.

The huge tent and the hundreds of people coming to the meetings fascinated me. I realized that I didn't have Pastor Cleveland's large staff of Bible workers to assist me, but surely I could have a few crumbs of blessings that fell from the Master's table.

I had never met Pastor Cleveland, but after two nights, I asked for an appointment to see him. I explained how I'd held meeting after meeting, trying to share the good news of God's amazing grace, but nothing seemed to happen. Few people came, and hardly any of those who did, accepted the Lord.

"Don't become discouraged, son," he sympathized, "for that's a tool of the devil." Then the older pastor promised, "God will lay His mighty hand on you—if you don't pull back."

As we knelt together, that dear man laid his hands on me. "Oh, my Father," he prayed, "I'm asking that You bless this servant of Yours as he works in Your vineyard. You said to ask for more workers in Your field, and Lord, here's one right in front of me. Brother Cox longs to bring Your saving truth to dying souls, and we know that it's not by might, nor by power, but only by Your Word and Your Spirit that men and women are drawn to Christ. So bless this dear brother, I pray, and breathe Your Spirit on him."

As we stood up, Pastor Cleveland advised, "Continue to throw yourself before the Lord; He won't always turn away from you."

This encounter settled the questions in my mind. I was going to work for the saving of souls for the rest of my life, and leave the results totally to the Lord.

With all my heart

The next meeting I held was in Raton, right on the state line between New Mexico and Colorado. The conference provided an air tent in which to hold the meetings, and we found a good location to pitch it.

Because it was summer, the conference had sent a teacher, Edgar Browning, to help with the meetings. And because it was so far from home, I rented a large old house to provide room for all those who would be helping us. As usual, the Lord had planned ahead, because the old house had just the number of rooms we needed!

Dewey Collins, my nonsmoking head deacon, had a son named Dan, who was known throughout the area as a troublemaker, and had been in just about every kind of trouble there was with the law. He'd wrecked several cars, spent time in jail, and was drunk most of the time, but he had been wonderfully converted at a camp meeting in Oklahoma City. Dan was on fire for the Lord and wanted to help advance His cause any way he could.

He was excited about our meetings in Raton and was helping to get everything ready, but then one day he disappeared—totally. No one seemed to know where he'd gone; but in a few days some of the folks came to me saying, "Have you heard about Dan? He's been drinking again."

"What do you mean?" I asked.

"Oh, he's really tied one on this time! He's been drunk for several days."

An entire week and several more days passed before Dan showed up. In he came—unshaven and dirty, a real mess. He hadn't bathed, and he'd slept in the same clothes for almost two weeks.

"Do you want to know where I've been?" he asked me.

"No."

"Do you want to know what I've been doing?"

"No."

"Well, what do you want to know?" he asked.

"Dan, do you still love the Lord?"

He hung his head and answered, "With all my heart."

"Well, then, go get cleaned up," I said.

From that day, Dan never looked back, and eventually he became a powerful evangelist for the Lord, winning thousands to Christ.

About that same time, I received a call from a young woman whose family, the Coulters, were members of the church in Clayton. Veleeta was a senior nursing student in Boulder, Colorado, and she and another young woman, Rosie Gardner, were to graduate in a few days. Both girls had been engaged to be married right after graduation, but both had been jilted by the young men to whom they were engaged.

Brokenhearted, they called me, sobbing as if their whole world had fallen out from under them.

"Why don't you come to Raton after graduation and help with the evangelistic meetings?" I asked. "You could give health lectures each night, and you'll be so busy you'll forget all about those two unworthy young men."

They agreed, and so the school teacher, Edgar Browning (along with his wife, Shirley, and their two children), Dan, who had just given up drinking, and Veleeta and Rosie all moved into the old house with my family.

The audience filled the tent from the first night, and what a team we had! Edgar took care of the music and helped with visitation. Dan did everything necessary at the tent and also worked at visitation. Veleeta and Rosie gave health lectures and made some visits. Marilyn and Shirley took care of the children who came, prepared meals for the crew, and helped with the organizational end of the meetings. I worked daily on my sermons and maintained a strong visitation program.

The rainmaker

During the last week, a man I'd never seen before came over to me after the meeting.

"Mr. Cox, I wonder if I might be able to rent this tent when you're done with it next week."

"This tent?" I asked, surprised.

"Yes, I've been driving by here every night and I've seen all the cars. I know that every night you take up an offering and make lots of money, so I'd like to rent the tent and give lectures on how to make rain. I figure if I take an offering, I could do real well."

The summer had been even drier than normal in the area, and the lake that supplied water for the city had dropped so low that water was rationed. In fact, the situation became so desperate that the city had hired a rainmaker to try to help fill up the lake!

Every day the rainmaker would take a tub to the top of the mountain and pour chemicals into it, stirring them vigorously, trying to make rain. Ironically, it rained all around Raton, but not in Raton! The city had given him $1,500 with the promise of another $1,500 if he could raise the lake by three inches, so for the entire month, while our meetings continued, he tried to make it rain—but it continued to be as dry as in the days of Elijah!

I knew I was talking to the rainmaker.

"I'm sorry, but this tent doesn't even belong to me," I explained. "In fact, I happen to know that it's already spoken for as soon as we finish our meetings. But my friend, I really don't think you want to go to the expense of renting a hall to try to make money lecturing on rainmaking! That could be pretty slow going!"

The rainmaker walked away unconvinced, and a few days later, I saw an ad in the paper announcing that he would be lecturing at the youth club.

Later I saw him coming down the street.

"Well, how did it go?" I asked, after exchanging pleasant greetings. "How many people came out to hear your lecture?"

"Three," he answered.

I couldn't help myself. "How much did you get in your offering?"

"Eleven cents."

How to marry a minister

The meetings I was holding moved much more smoothly than previous ones had, and God blessed with a baptism of twenty-five people. On the last day, our small crew took down the tent and packed everything away. It had been a full day, and we would all be parting the next morning.

Marilyn and I had already gone to bed when there was a knock on our door. It was Veleeta and Rosie.

"Come on in, girls!" Marilyn said.

The two young women came in and sat down on the edge of the bed.

"We've been thinking," they began. "We've enjoyed helping with the meetings so much that we've decided we want to marry ministers. So tell us what we need to do."

"Well, I don't know how to tell you to marry a minister," I began, "but I guess if you want to marry one you'll need to go where the ministers are. Both of you have a profession, so I'd suggest you go to the seminary, get a job nearby, and take some of the same classes the ministers take. That way you'll get acquainted with some of the young, eligible ministers."

Off to the seminary Veleeta went, and sure enough, she met a young man studying for the ministry and married him! Rosie received an invitation to be the school nurse at Southwestern Union College, which she accepted. But more on her story later.

Ordination

Things were going well in our district, and I was convinced that

Marilyn and Kenneth

God's guiding hand was over our ministry. During camp meeting at Sandia View Academy near Albuquerque, I was to be ordained to the gospel ministry. Pastor L. C. Evans, the president of the Southwestern Union, had the ordination service. I was the only one ordained, and I remember feeling humbled and unworthy of such an honor. It was totally unexpected, and I heard of the plan only a week or so before the ordination took place.

As people came up and expressed their congratulations, my thoughts were on surrender. Surrendering my all to the Lord—asking Him to guide my life.

We spent almost five years in the Texas Panhandle, and the people we worked with became dear friends. We looked forward to continuing our ministry among them, but then our conference president called.

"Brother Kenneth?"

"Yes?" I said, with a little hesitation.

"The conference committee has just met, and we want to invite you to become the pastor of the Albuquerque Central church."

I was surprised. I had worked in that church as an intern under Pastor Harold Richards five years before, and now they were asking me to pastor the largest church in the conference. I believed that I should watch for the Lord's leading in my life, and when the conference committee met and prayed concerning where I was to work in the Lord's vineyard, I needed to listen. But this was a bolt out of the blue. It was not something that I had expected or had any idea would happen. I certainly didn't want to go against the Lord's will, but I was afraid. I could relate to Moses when the Lord called him into service. Going from a church of fifty members to one of this size was intimidating. All I could do was fall on my knees and pray, *Lord, give me the wisdom and ability to do Your will.*

Chapter 12

Three Mighty Men and a Bachelor

"He performs wonders that cannot be fathomed,
miracles that cannot be counted."

—Job 9:10, NIV

A lot had changed in five years. A lot of spiritual growth had taken place in our family, as well as growth in the amount of furniture and belongings! We were learning daily to depend more deeply on the Lord, seeking His guidance in every situation. But the Albuquerque church was in a state of shock when we arrived. Lyle Pollett, one of the young men who led out in music ministry, played the organ, and was active in church leadership, had come home one day to find his young wife lying on the couch—dead! She'd just delivered a baby a few days before, and some of the medicine she had been taking had caused a fatal reaction. The women in the church took care of the baby and helped as much as possible while Lyle tried to pull his life back together. At this time I got a close, refreshing look at a church that seemed to have a heart like God's. Those members loved each other and were willing to be there whenever there was a need. Little did I realize just how committed they were to serving God!

Marilyn and I spent the first few months getting acquainted with the members while settling into our new responsibilities. The church was full when we arrived, and before long it became necessary to have two services on Sabbath due to the additional people who began attending. That worked for a while, but the Sabbath School rooms became hopelessly crowded. The church just needed more room, so what should we do? We could build a bigger church, or we could start a new church in the northeastern part of Albuquerque.

Twins

One evening Lyle came to our home and told us that one of the couples in the church had given him the name of a young lady. "We've been corresponding over the last few months, and I'm becoming quite interested in her," he said. "But I don't want to make a mistake, so I need some unbiased advice. Would you please look at some of her letters and tell me what you think?"

"What's her name, Lyle?" I asked.

"Her name is Rosie, and she's the school nurse at Southwestern Union College."

"No kidding!" I laughed. "Lyle, I don't need to look at the letters. I probably know Rosie better than you do! She's a fine young woman."

The romance continued, and I had the privilege of marrying them. A few months later, they came over to visit.

"Kenneth, I've been praying long and hard about it, and I've decided to go back to school and study for the ministry," Lyle said.

And so it was that both Veleeta and Rosie married ministers, and both gave birth to twins! The Lord leads in mysterious ways, His wonders to perform.

"Your steel is ready"

A group of members at the Albuquerque Central church eventually formed a new church in the northeastern part of the city and called themselves the Heights church. In preparation for building, they rented from a Protestant church not far from their purchased land and began looking for an architect to draw up plans for their new church.

Paul Lawrence, a plumber who had lost his job some time earlier because of accepting Jesus Christ, was one of the big movers in pushing for a new church. He had started his own plumbing business, working out of his garage, and by the time we moved to Albuquerque, he owned a very large and successful plumbing company. He pledged to be responsible for the heating and air conditioning for the new church.

The little group pulled together all their ideas for the new church and submitted them to the architect. Now they were anxious for the plans to come back, so they could get started. When the full plans arrived, we were eager to get them out for bid so we'd know what it would actually cost to build. But alas! Even the lowest bid was far more money than they had.

I was still young and probably overly optimistic. My only experience was building the little church in Clayton, but I would not be deterred.

"Let's just contract it ourselves. We have enough builders in the church. We can do this!" I told my church members. Had it not been for Paul's wise counsel and help, there's no telling what kind of building we would have ended up with!

We put out the bid for excavating the foundation and for the floor. Again, all the bids that came back were for more money than we had.

"That's OK," I said, "We'll do it ourselves!"

I still marvel at the men who took on such a tremendous load to help build their beloved church bit by bit, most of them knowing— far better than I did—just how much work would be involved!

One day I was down in the ditch, tying rebar for the foundation, when a car drove up. A fellow I didn't recognize got out and came over.

"Hello, there!" the man said in a friendly manner. "I understand you're going to build a church here."

"Yes, sir."

"Could I take a look at your blueprints?"

"Sure," I said, handing them over. I went back to tying rebar, and after a bit, the man came over again.

"I notice the plans call for some structural steel beams," he commented. "What are you going to do for steel?"

"I don't know," I answered truthfully.

The man cleared his throat. "How are you going to get the steel for the church?" he asked again.

"Oh, we're just going to buy the steel and fabricate it ourselves," I said, drawing on my vast store of inexperience.

He looked at me for a moment. "Do you have any shop drawings?"

Since I didn't know what shop drawings were, I answered, "No, sir."

"Well, if you'll lend me a set of your blueprints, I'll get you a set of shop drawings," he said. "Will you take a donation for the church?"

"Why sure, we'd be happy to accept it."

Writing out a check for five hundred dollars, he took the blueprints and left!

With the excavation finally finished, the foundations and floor were poured. We were just about ready for the structural steel when my phone rang.

"Sir, we have the steel for your church, and we're ready to bring it out," said the voice on the line.

"Excuse me," I said, "I think you must have the wrong number."

"Are you building the church on Wyoming Street?" he asked.

"Yes, but I didn't order any steel, so don't bring anything out and dump it on our land because we can't pay for it."

"Sir, the steel is all paid for," he replied.

I was stunned speechless. The man who had taken our blueprints had ordered the steel—*and paid for it*!

Now I was really excited! The next Sabbath I told the church what happened.

"I want every man and woman to come out tomorrow because we're going to work on the church!" I said. And the congregation turned out in force.

Now it's one thing to have miraculous steel beams lying on the ground beside your proposed new church, but it's quite another to figure out how to get them off the ground and up where they belong!

All the men and women stood around, looking at the steel. Then they looked up at the sky where it needed to be lifted. Some even ventured to try to lift one end—unsuccessfully, of course.

"I think we'd better pray," I said.

As we finished our prayer, we heard a distant rumbling sound. Every eye turned toward the road, and our mouths hung open as two gigantic cranes turned into our lot! By sundown every beam was in place!

The stranger's gift to us included putting the steel beams he had donated into place. I have often marveled at how the Lord impresses human hearts.

Three mighty men

When it was time for the blocks and brick to go up, God was again true to His promise, "Before they call, I will answer" (Isaiah 65:24, KJV). He already had another man in line to step up to the plate.

Ken Thompson was raised in Keene, Texas, by a godly Adventist mother. When he moved to Albuquerque, he started working as a brick mason. The man he worked for took a liking to him, and before he died, he put Ken in a position to take over his company. When I moved to the area, Ken had the largest masonry business in New Mexico. He was so good at it and worked his program so well, that to this day, his bricklaying is still a standard for other buildings in that state.

Ken was a generous man and helped us tremendously. But although his wife and daughter were members of our church, he had never felt he could become a church member and still run his business. Now God impressed him to take his masonry crew and lay the block and bricks for the church.

This story reminds me of David's three mighty men. The Bible says in 2 Samuel 23:13–17,

> Then three of the thirty chief men went down at harvest time and came to David at the cave of Adullam. And the troop of Philistines encamped in the Valley of Rephaim. David was then in the stronghold, and the garrison of the Philistines was then in Bethlehem. And David said with longing, "Oh, that someone would give me a drink of the water from the well of Bethlehem, which is by the gate!" So the three mighty men broke through the camp of the Philistines, drew water from the well of Bethlehem that was by the gate, and took it and brought it to David. Nevertheless he would not drink it, but poured it out to the LORD. And he said, "Far be it from me, O LORD, that I should do this! Is this not the blood of the men who went in jeopardy of their lives?" Therefore he would not drink it. These things were done by the three mighty men (NKJV).

The third "mighty man," and chief among them in Albuquerque, was Blake Chanslor. Heaven only knows what all this man did for the cause of God over the years! Blake was most generous, and put up enormous amounts to help build churches. He owned a chain of hamburger stands and was a very astute businessman. But he also had a heart for God and a burden to help the Lord's work. He was a special blessing to me over the years, not only by his financial support, but also as a friend and a counselor. He was very, very helpful.

Blake covered all the expenses for the electrical needs of the church, from the wiring to the light fixtures. Then time and time again, he pulled the congregation out of trouble by giving or supplying something they needed for the church.

Because of the three "mighty men" of Albuquerque, and many other members and friends who allowed the Lord to impress and use them, today you can drive out on Wyoming Street in Northeast Albu-querque and see a church that *God* built! Our heavenly Father has a thousand ways of providing that we could never dream of.

A can of corn

Don Young, a shy, eccentric bachelor who lived alone, was a mem-ber of the Albuquerque Central church. He didn't waste a lot of time cleaning and tidying himself or his surroundings, and he drove an old car whose interior strongly resembled a trash can on wheels. However, he came faithfully to church and was readily accepted by the warm-hearted members.

One Sabbath I was standing at the door shaking hands as the con-gregation left the worship service, and as Don shook my hand, he asked quietly, "Would you come home with me for lunch?"

His request caught me totally by surprise, but I answered, "Why, sure, Don, I'd be happy to."

Marilyn was standing nearby, so I whispered to her, "You take the children on home. I'm going to go have lunch with Don."

His house was almost bare, containing only the sparsest of furni-ture. I honestly wasn't sure what I'd gotten myself into because as I entered, I didn't see or smell anything cooking in the kitchen.

"Have a seat and I'll be back in a little bit," Don said as he left the room. A few minutes later, he walked into the dining room with two open cans of corn, a spoon stuck in each one. He handed me a can and kept the other for himself.

"Let's have the blessing," he said.

We thanked God for the food and started eating.

"How's the new church coming along?" he asked.

I explained the progress that had been made, along with how God had miraculously blessed our efforts. "But our challenges aren't over yet," I added. "The members who are actually moving to the new church aren't the wealthiest in the world, and the financial burden of building has turned out to be a lot more than we had anticipated. But

God is blessing, and I know He'll provide in His own way and time."

Don listened attentively. "I'd like to help on the church," he offered quietly.

"Why, that's very thoughtful of you, Don. We always appreciate any help."

He got up and went into his bedroom, returning in a few minutes with a check.

"Thank you so much, Don," I said, as I stuck the check in my pocket. "We always receive a blessing when we share in the work of God."

After we finished visiting, I started driving home and remembered the check. I pulled off the road to fish it out of my pocket. This proved to be a wise move; otherwise, I might have wrecked the car. The check was for *twenty thousand dollars*!

After the shock wore off a bit, I asked myself, *I wonder if this check is good?* But when I called Don's bank on Monday morning, I discovered it was good. No, it was *very good*!

I mused at the number of times when unusual people like Don are treated as if they have no value. God reminded me that each person is of infinite value in His eyes—whether they have money to give to His cause or not. After all, He would still have given His Son—even if only *one soul,* however eccentric, had fallen into sin!

Because I'd spent so much time building the church, I had not been able to hold any evangelistic meetings in the south valley of Albuquerque as I had hoped. My heart burned to become more involved in direct soul winning, and I remember feeling uneasy, as if I needed to be about my Father's business.

Chapter 13

Gasping for Air

Behold, the LORD's hand is not shortened, that it cannot save;
neither his ear heavy, that it cannot hear.

—Isaiah 59:1, KJV

We had spent ten years in the Texico Conference, and though it had been a time of growth and maturing, I wondered what the Lord had in mind for us next. I loved being a pastor, and the time I spent working with my churches was a joy. Each member was special, but I wasn't totally sure that I was following God's will for my life. Within my soul was a constant desire to tell others about Jesus, along with the message that I knew was to be given before His return.

Cyril Miller, who had worked with me during our evangelistic meetings in Dalhart, Texas, was now president of the Chesapeake Conference of Seventh-day Adventists, which included Maryland, Delaware, and part of West Virginia. He invited me to become Sabbath School and Lay Activities director for the Chesapeake Conference. I had felt for some time that lay members have great soul-winning possibilities, though little was being done to harness their potential. Cyril also mentioned his desire to hold evangelistic meetings, and he assured me I would be able to conduct as many as I wished—in addition to my other duties. This opened the way for me to do what I believed the Lord was calling me to do, so, with great anticipation, I accepted the call.

He's lost!

One of the responsibilities assigned me was superintendency of the Chesapeake Conference camp meeting, an annual summer church event across the United States. Camp meetings have always given me a sense of excitement—hundreds of people coming in to spend the week studying God's Word and worshiping together. All the ministers from the churches throughout Maryland and Delaware would be arriving to prepare the campground. Many people would be living in tents, so there would be hundreds pitched, in addition to the large tents for various meetings.

Laura, Jimmy, Marilyn, and Kenneth

Somehow in the busyness of getting the children to their meetings and attending meetings ourselves, Marilyn and I suddenly realized that Jimmy was nowhere to be found. He was gone! He had truly disappeared.

"Calm down, Marilyn," I said. "We'll find him in just a few minutes." But my heart was in my throat as I began to pray.

At first just Marilyn, Laura, and I hurried through the encampment and out to the surrounding areas that might be tempting to a little boy. After some time with no success, I enlisted the help of some other ministers. The search continued for almost two hours! Others prayed for Jimmy's safety, but no one could remember seeing the boy.

"Jimmy? Jimmy!" we called, but he didn't answer us.

Most families were staying in tents, which were pitched in rows on the academy grounds. Suddenly, as I glanced at a tent with a partially opened flap, I thought I spotted a familiar leg on someone's bed. Backing up and cautiously opening the tent flap further, I was greatly relieved to see my young son sound asleep—oblivious to our anxiety.

"I was tired, Daddy," Jimmy explained as I gathered him into my arms. "I found this bed, and nobody else was here, so I thought it would be OK to take a nap."

Relieved that Jimmy was OK, we thanked the Lord and were able to calm our hearts so we could be blessed by the meeting that afternoon.

The gas fiasco

A lot was happening in the Chesapeake Conference. Cyril, Bill May, and Joe Crews had started a radio program called *Amazing Facts,* and it was growing fast. After I arrived, I became involved in getting numerous *Amazing Facts* folders written, printed, and circulated. Life took on a fast pace, and though I was still working for the Lord, it was simply not as rewarding to me as working with individuals and sharing the gospel. I began to feel disconnected—I was still there, but on the sidelines. I was giving directions, instead of working face-to-face with interested people.

This feeling was short lived, however, once I began to pray about it. I was impressed that I should begin conducting evangelistic meetings myself. Soon I was back in the pulpit, feeling connected. I was back to having direct contact with men and women and telling them about Jesus Christ. That was my calling, my passion.

I worked in the Chesapeake Conference for four years, holding meetings throughout the area. We used an air tent again for the meetings in Charlestown, West Virginia, because these portable buildings were very adaptable and could be set up on a vacant lot when a suitable building could not be rented.

But air tents came with their challenges! In preparation for one of the events, the church members and I worked hard making the inside as nice as any building. We carpeted the floor, purchased live plants for the platform, and moved in a piano and organ. Because the weather had turned cold, it was necessary to heat the tent, but this was really no problem because huge fans kept the air moving constantly in order to hold the tent up.

Some of the mothers had placed their babies in car seats on the floor beside their chairs, and while I was preaching one night I noticed a couple of them take their children outside because they were crying. I felt a little peculiar, even though I was concentrating intently on my closing points. Gradually, I became aware that I was having trouble picking up my feet—in fact, I could hardly lift them off the platform!

When Pastor Larry Boggess came forward to give the closing prayer, I whispered to him, "Are you feeling all right?"

"No, not very good," he answered.

At the end of the prayer, I was immediately back at the microphone.

"Stay seated, everyone. Please remain seated!" I said. "Something unusual has happened here, and you need to carefully follow these instructions. The ventilation system for our heaters has apparently malfunctioned, and the fans have sent carbon monoxide into the tent."

There was a sharp gasp from the audience.

"We are obviously all OK, though, because no one is unconscious," I reassured them. "But you need to get up very slowly and walk out as orderly as possible. And I want to assure you that everything will be corrected and safe before tomorrow night's meeting!"

The crowd stood to their feet to follow the instructions, and twenty people promptly passed out! We immediately called the hospital, and ambulances came screaming to the site. Eighteen people were taken to the hospital that night, and I went with them to inform the medical staff that I would be responsible for their hospital bills. Sixteen individuals were treated and sent home, and two stayed overnight and were discharged the next day.

The local newspaper splashed the unfortunate happening across the morning headlines, and my heart sank. I knew the newspaper article would probably be a deathblow to the meetings, not to mention what the people who were there would tell their neighbors!

And then there was the hospital bill! *How can I even begin to pay for eighteen emergency room visits?* I wondered. I imagined the devil laughing with hellish glee, but the following night the crowd at the air tent was bigger than ever before!

The hospital sent me a bill for eighteen dollars, and how we thanked God for His care—and for the kindness of the medical and billing staff at the hospital!

A bug in a snowdrift

Cyril Miller accepted a call to be secretary of the Southwestern Union and, with his transfer, Bill May became president of the Chesapeake Conference. With the change in leadership, my responsibilities increased as well; now I was asked to coordinate all the evangelism for the conference.

That should be right down my alley—correct?

Wrong!

The job I had hoped would increase my opportunity to bring people to Jesus through evangelism now had me sitting on more committees than ever before! Oh, how I longed just to talk to someone about the Lord! Sometimes, after sitting in committees all day, I would go to the Bible store, purchase some tracts, and pass them out door-to-door.

That April I was invited to attend a convention held by the General Conference for lay activities directors in Banff, Canada, so Marilyn and I decided to drive, making a bit of a vacation out of it. We arranged for Laura to stay with friends so she wouldn't miss school, and Marilyn, Jimmy, and I packed ourselves—and all our luggage—into our little Volkswagen.

We decided to stop in Jamestown, North Dakota, to see Marilyn's cousin, Judy Kruger. When we left Washington, D.C., the world was alive with blooming trees and flowers. However, by the time we reached Jamestown, we were in the midst of a serious blizzard! We decided to stop for gas because Judy lived ten miles out of town. When we got back on the road, the snow was falling so thick and fast that I couldn't even see the road!

I rolled down the window, stuck my head out, and finally saw what I believed to be the road leading to her house. Turning in, though, the road just fell out from underneath us! We sank into a frozen, immovable pile of snow—stuck fast and unable to get out.

Leaving the lights on, I walked up the road as far as I could without losing sight of the car lights. No sign of Judy's house. Coming back to the car, I said, "I'm afraid we're going to have to spend the night in the car. It's a good thing we got gas back in Jamestown! I hope it will last all night."

With the blankets Marilyn had packed, and by huddling together, we were able to survive the night. We prayed earnestly for God's protection, realizing how dangerous our predicament was. *What if while we sleep, the snow piles up around the car enough to choke off the tailpipe?* We knew that the carbon monoxide coming into the vehicle would kill us all—silently and without warning!

By morning's first light, the storm had ended. When I got out to survey the situation, I found a space of about two feet all around the car where the snow had not piled up. Beyond that, the snow was two to three feet deep in every direction! We were on the right road all right, but the dip in the road had been too deep for the car to make it through. There, about three hundred yards up the road, was the Krugers' house! The Lord had cared for us through the night! We praised Him for His protection.

Because the cows were calving, we spent the day in the pasture, picking up newborn calves and putting them in the basement so they wouldn't freeze to death. By the time the day was over, the basement was full of calves. The next day we said our reluctant Goodbyes to the Krugers and headed north.

Banff in the winter is spectacular, and the conference was held in a large chalet with breathtaking views. One evening as we sat in the lobby chatting, Fernon Retzer, a Sabbath School director at the General Conference, began talking about something he'd recently seen demonstrated. I was immediately interested, and Fernon said, "Just a minute—I'll show you."

He set up two projectors and two screens side by side, running them both simultaneously, explaining how one could give a multimedia presentation. At that time no one had ever heard of putting more than one picture at a time in front of people. How could they possibly watch more than one picture?

But the idea clicked with me as I imagined illustrating sermons much more effectively using multiple projectors. In fact, from that point on, the idea absolutely took over my mind, and I could hardly wait to try it out! But Jimmy was begging to go tobogganing, so I took a bit of time out for that. After all, with so much snow and beauty around, it would have been a shame to spend all my time indoors! We had a great afternoon together.

Multimedia

Upon our return home, I began looking for anything I could find about multimedia. One Sunday I saw a full-page ad in the newspaper for a trade show of audio-visual equipment. I was sure they would have something on the use of multiple projectors—and I couldn't get down there fast enough!

"May I see your pass, please?" the guard at the door asked.

"Uh, I don't have a pass," I replied, "but since this was in the paper, I thought it was for anyone."

"I'm sorry, but no one is allowed in without a pass or proof of dealership," he replied.

"Listen, I don't mind paying—"

"Sorry, you must have a pass."

"I'm a minister, and I'm really interested in multimedia to—"

"Sir, I'm sorry, but you *must* have a pass."

I realized it was useless to argue, so I headed back home a very disappointed man. On the way, I stopped by the offices of the Columbia Union of Seventh-day Adventists, and Pastor Mort Julberg happened to be in. Woefully, I related to him what had happened at the trade show.

Then, rather innocently, Mort asked, "How badly do you want to go?" And with a twinkle in his eye, he pulled out a couple of press passes.

"Come on, let's go!" he said.

Multimedia was *the* big, new thing—at least as far as I was concerned. For the next three days, I went to the trade show and marveled at all the new ideas. I picked up material, then went home and read it late into the night. By the time the trade show was over, I knew exactly what I wanted!

This conviction grew in me as the days and weeks went by. In fact, it was all I could think about! My desire had been to lead men and women to Christ, but now the Lord impressed me more than ever that I should get into full-time soul winning. Of course, this would be a big decision, and I needed to be sure my family was with me. Marilyn said she would support me in whatever I decided, but now I needed to be sure that this was indeed the Lord's leading and not merely my own interest. I knew I wanted to go into full-time evangelism, but where? And when?

Finally, I went in and told Bill May, my conference president, that I was leaving.

"Where are you going?" Bill asked.

"Well, I don't know, but I know that I'm leaving."

"What are you going to do?" he pressed.

"I'm going into full-time evangelism."

"Where? Which conference?"

"I don't know, but I'm going," was all I could say, knowing it didn't make any more sense to Bill than it did to my own family. *It didn't even make a lot of sense to me.* I just had a strong conviction that I must follow the Lord's leading.

I didn't tell anyone else. I just prayed—*a lot*—and waited.

Committed

Meanwhile, Cyril Miller, who was now secretary of the Southwestern Union, was sitting on the platform at the Oklahoma camp meeting with Connie Skantz, president of the Oklahoma Conference.

"What are you doing in evangelism this year, Connie?" he whispered.

"Not much," he answered. "We just don't have the money."

"How much do you need?"

"I would imagine at least fifty thousand dollars to hire an evangelist and pay for the meeting expenses."

"Will you let me have fifteen minutes?" Cyril asked.

"Go ahead. See what you can do."

Cyril got up and began telling the people that there was no money to do evangelism in their conference. "The Great Commission—the only commission Jesus gave us—was to preach the gospel to every creature—*including those in the Oklahoma Conference,*" he said. "If we can raise fifty thousand dollars today to hire an evangelist and pay for the meetings, I believe I can get Pastor Kenneth Cox to come be your evangelist."

Cyril hadn't talked with me, and as far as I knew, he did not know of my conviction. But God did, and that day the Adventists in Oklahoma gave more than fifty thousand dollars.

The phone at our house rang. "I've just committed you to be the evangelist for the Oklahoma Conference," Cyril said matter-of-factly.

"Praise God!" I responded, "When do I start?"

Who could have asked for a more direct answer from the Lord?

Chapter 14

Playing With Fire

When thou walkest through the fire, thou shalt not be burned;
neither shall the flame kindle upon thee.
—*Isaiah 43:2, KJV*

Moving to Oklahoma City gave Marilyn the precious opportunity to be close to her parents. It also allowed our children, Laura and Jimmy, a special bonding time with their grandparents and other relatives. In addition, it was also near where I was reared. I knew the territory—and the people even spoke my language!

The one thing I lacked in my work, though, was projection equipment for my evangelistic meetings. I knew what I wanted, but new ideas are hard to sell, so I went to the bank and borrowed fifteen thousand dollars.

I decided to use four rear projection screens together to look like one massive screen. I would need two projectors for each screen so text could be superimposed on the illustrations; that meant I really needed *eight* projectors. Buying the equipment was the easy part—but getting slides to illustrate each point was a different story!

Of course, those were the days before computer imaging and projection, so a black background with white lettering was required to superimpose text on another slide. But nothing like that existed at the time. So I used a little ingenuity by typing the text onto a white sheet of paper and then taking a photograph of it. The negative gave me a black background with white letters—exactly what I wanted, and it looked great! But when I put the slide into the projector, it enlarged exponentially on the screen, revealing very jagged edges, which were much too distracting to use.

I went through a dozen processes, including hand setting the text, but nothing seemed to work. Finally, I found a printer, Noble Vining, who said he could do it, and when we took a picture of his work, thankfully, the letters were straight.

The next job was to find colored pictures to illustrate my sermons. We tried using pictures out of books, but when they were enlarged, they looked grainy and blurred. It didn't take me long to realize that if I was going to have a quality presentation, I needed to take pictures of the original artwork. I contacted the manager of the Southern Publishing Association and explained what I was trying to accomplish.

"Would you let us come there and take pictures of your original artwork?" I asked. "It's the only way we can get the quality we need for large-screen projection."

The gracious manager allowed us to take pictures of all the artwork in their archives!

Next, I contacted the Review and Herald® Publishing Association and explained what I was doing.

"Oh, no, I'm sorry," was their response. "We can't allow these paintings to be photographed because they are all copyrighted. We understand what you're trying to do, but we have contracts with our artists."

And so it was that I photographed artwork at Forest Lawn Cemetery in California, Oral Roberts University, in Tulsa, Oklahoma, and at several other publishing houses.

However, God has a way of working things out, and after some time a new manager came to the Review and Herald®. He was sympathetic to what we were trying to accomplish and invited me to come in and photograph any artwork I could use in bringing people to Christ.

Upon entering the art vaults at Review and Herald®, I could hardly believe my eyes. *There must be more artwork here than in the Vatican!* I thought. What wonderful treasures I found to illustrate the great truths of God's Word! Here were beautiful pictures, painted by fantastic artists to illustrate one point in a book—but then their work was put in a vault, never to be seen again!

While I was photographing these paintings in the art department, everything went smoothly. But I couldn't help but notice the truly great pictures hanging in the halls and in various offices! I was given permission to remove them and take them to the art department, photograph them, and return them to their original locations. But this procedure soon caused me trouble, as I quickly realized that many of the employees at the Review wondered what this stranger was doing! Why was he taking away their precious paintings?

While I was taking a picture off a wall in the hall, several men or their secretaries would come out of their offices.

"Who told you to take that picture?" they would ask, or, "Where are you taking it?"

Some went even further. "You can't take that picture!" they would say emphatically.

Finally, the manager assigned an employee to escort me in order to reassure the others that I was authorized to remove the paintings.

After photographing the artwork at Review and Herald®, I was also allowed to photograph the artwork at Pacific Press®. Now, with thousands of wonderful pictures in hand, I could illustrate each nightly presentation effectively.

Museum meetings

My first evangelistic meetings in Oklahoma were held in Claremore, at the Will Rogers Memorial Museum. The curator agreed to rent the building, but instructed me not to move the life-sized wax figures depicting the Lord's Supper backstage. Because I was using rearview projection, I placed the screens in front of the table, with the projectors behind the wax figures. I definitely remember feeling a bit uneasy each night as I walked across the Lord's table to change slide trays and adjust my projectors.

Certainly it was the grace of God alone that made that series successful. With eight projectors, I had a button for each projector to move it forward or backward, in addition to a button to move them all forward, and another one to move them all backward at once! It was challenging, to say the least! With ten buttons on the pulpit, my sermon notes were covered with circled numbers indicating which projector to change and what button to push! I figured that with two buttons, I had a 50 percent chance of making a mistake, but with each additional button the odds multiplied—always against me! Of course, I also had to keep preaching, watch for my audience's responses, and not lose track of my notes. Though I was very much aware of the Holy Spirit's guidance, I soon realized I needed something, or someone *other than me,* to control the projectors. I liked to walk from one side of the platform to the other while preaching—but now I was tied to the pulpit. I found it hard to speak when I couldn't walk.

Essentially, I'd been doing evangelism alone—with a lot of help from Marilyn, of course. But now I realized I was in extreme need of more help. Attendance at the meetings was good, but that meant a lot of visitation had to be done. The additional stress of keeping up with my visual presentations stretched me very thin. I began to pray.

One night after the meeting, Bill and Betty Sorensen came up. "Pastor, could you use any help? We'd like to lend a hand with these meetings, if you don't think we'd be in the way."

Could I use some help?

"Has God been speaking to you?" I asked. "I could use a dozen helpers if I had them!"

Bill and Betty were building houses, but decided to get up at 4:00 A.M. to work on their construction project. Then at noon they would come over and help me! What a great blessing they were. After the meetings were over, they even started helping prepare for the next series. I will never forget my first full-time evangelistic team: Bill and Betty Sorensen, Marilyn, and me!

Fire!

About this time, a new piece of hardware came out that would operate multiple projectors at the same time. I purchased the machine, and because it was midwinter (a downtime for evangelistic meetings in Oklahoma), I decided to program all my presentations onto it. I needed a lot of space to lay all my slides out, so I got permission to use a large room behind the auditorium at the conference campground. There was no heat in the building, so I borrowed a butane heater and set up shop. I brought in about twenty slide viewers and laid out thousands of slides so I could see everything I had. The new programmer was a punch tape machine with little contact points on a cogwheel. When I pressed a button, the wheel turned, and the contact points made contact through the hole I'd punched in the tape. This caused the projector to advance—at least in theory.

The gizmo could operate ten projectors and seemed so simple. However, I admit to literally lying on the floor and crying over that thing! When I would call the company about my problems, they'd say, "You know as much about it as we do—maybe more!" So I labored and prayed over that first set of presentations. I could almost imagine the imps and demons trying to thwart my efforts to make the Word of God clear.

One day, while I was working diligently, the butane tank suddenly exploded. Immediately fire was everywhere, enveloping me—and everything else in the room! The heat was unbelievable, but thinking only of the loss of my hard work, I threw my coat over the heater and tank, dragging them outside—burning my hands severely in the process.

The plastic curtains on the windows melted, the plastic slide viewers with their cardboard stands curled up, and some of the cardboard even caught fire. But as I surveyed the damage, I found that not much else was hurt! Because the slides were gravity-fed into the projectors, I had decided to use glass mounts to avoid jamming problems. The glass was heavy enough to fall, eliminating the danger of the slides jamming inside the projector. As it turned out, this also helped to protect them, as well. The Lord's hand had certainly been over it all.

A prayer of thanksgiving went up to my heavenly Father. I was keenly aware that this could have been the end, not only of all my hard-won pictures and equipment, but also of the camp meeting auditorium—and perhaps of my own life!

While many supported and encouraged me in what I was attempting, others scoffed at the idea and insisted it would never work. Another evangelist even made a special trip to tell me that my idea was a mistake and that it was draining time and money from preaching the gospel. But I persevered, and God blessed with fruitful meetings.

God knew his heart

Early one morning in 1972, I received a phone call from my sister Billie.

"Kenneth, Dad had a heart attack last night, and he didn't survive."

I met my grieving family in Hartshorne, Oklahoma, and what a sad time it was. How I wished I could have talked with my father about God's merciful love, but he would always become defensive and angry if I mentioned God. Perhaps someone else had been able to minister to him in that way, but all I could do now was to trust my loving, heavenly Father as we committed Dad's body to the earth.

Over the years, Dad's heart had softened. When we were children, he had always treated us like slaves, but once we were grown and came to visit, he treated us like his kids. He especially loved his grandkids.

When someone dies, there's a tendency to remember the good and forget the bad. That was true with Dad. I remembered the good times I had had with him. I loved him, but it pained me that he had rejected the Sabbath and all that he had learned. That seemed to be a turning point with him. I don't ever remember him having much to say or do with religion after that, but I didn't know his heart.

Dad had been married to his second wife, Bess, for eighteen years before he died at age seventy-two. He was the only boy of his family and had six sisters. I remember him often saying, "I have six sisters, and every one of them has a brother!"

Dad Otto Cox, Laura, Marilyn, and Kenneth

I am thankful that God is not trying to keep us out of heaven, but to get us into heaven. Therefore, even though my heart was heavy and sad, I could rest confidently in His mercy. I pushed aside all unpleasant memories, forgiven long before, remembering the good days— even as I prayed for God's mercy.

"He's going to kill you!"

Bill and Betty Sorensen eventually left us to pastor a church, and I found myself without a team. This left me in great need of help, not only for visitation, but also for organizing the meetings each night. They had grown to be very valuable workers and would be greatly missed.

Meanwhile, the conference had asked me to hold a meeting in Pauls Valley, Oklahoma, in hopes of starting a Seventh-day Adventist church there. Among those attending was a young woman named JoAnn, who had been raised in a church that taught that if you married, you could never divorce. They had told her that if she ever did remarry, she would be living in adultery, and that the only way to return to the Lord was to leave her second spouse and return to the first one! JoAnn was struggling with all of this because she had previously been married and divorced, and was now with her second husband.

Unaware of her mind-set on this matter, toward the end of the meeting, I made a call for those who would like to give their hearts to the Lord and follow Him in baptism to come forward. JoAnn came forward, along with several others, but kept quiet about her beliefs, returning home that evening to tell her husband Goodbye!

"I've given my heart to the Lord, so I can no longer be married to you," she told him. "I must go back to my first husband."

Well, this was all news to JoAnn's husband! He left the house in a rage, went to a bar, and began drinking. The only person he could think to blame for this was the preacher she'd been listening to! The drunker he got, the angrier and more irrational his thinking became. Finally, he decided he would just kill the preacher, so the next evening he went home, got his rifle, and headed for our meetings.

JoAnn learned of his intentions and became nearly hysterical! She managed to get to the meeting before he did and explained to me what was going on.

"My husband is on his way over here, and he's going to kill you!" she said.

It probably would have made anyone uneasy to get up alone on the platform in front of a large crowd while knowing he was the target of an armed and out-of-control man that night. So before stepping on the platform, I prayed even more earnestly than usual, committing my life to the Lord and entreating Him to handle the situation.

I believe that God asks only that we commit our ways to Him, and then He handles the circumstances. An elderly couple on their way to the meeting that evening had just come to a stoplight when the drunken husband pulled up right behind them in his pickup. When the light turned green, they didn't move immediately, so he blew the horn—loud and long. The elderly driver was so startled he stalled his car! That made the angry husband even angrier. He got out of his pickup and started beating on the frightened couple's windshield! As it shattered, a crowd gathered and the police were called. JoAnn's husband never made it to the meeting that night, but was hauled off to jail instead.

The next day I visited him in jail. We discussed what had taken place and finally he understood. The elderly couple didn't press charges, and I was able to bring about reconciliation between JoAnn and her husband. By God's grace I was still alive too!

Traffic jam

Long before we pray, God is working on an answer. I was in great need of help for the meetings. Melvin and Allene Weber had been members of the Dalhart church during the early days of my ministry. Melvin had built several assisted-living centers and nursing homes, which he managed. He also served as hospital administrator in Dalhart, so in addition to being personable

Top: Melvin Weber and Kenneth Cox
Bottom: Allene Weber and Marilyn Cox

and organized, he had great visitation skills. Allene had a beautiful voice, was very outgoing, and loved to entertain. Their children grown, they had just sold their nursing home in Plainview, Texas, and were looking for an opportunity to serve the Lord.

I had been praying for help with music for the meetings as well as in other areas, and we all felt that the Lord had directly answered our prayers in connecting us. The Webers proved to be a valuable addition to our team.

The largest meetings I conducted in Oklahoma were in Tulsa with pastor Gary Grimes. People came in such numbers that two sessions were held each night. The resulting traffic jam required the city to supply a policeman to direct traffic. Near the end of the meetings, Gary and I visited twenty-one homes and received twenty-one decisions to join the church in one day!

Word got out about what was happening, and outside guests began showing up, including the president of the Kentucky-Tennessee Conference. After the meeting one night, he came up to me and introduced himself, along with the other men with him. They expressed an interest in what I was doing, asking numerous questions about the multimedia equipment and how it all worked.

The Tulsa meeting ended with a large number of baptisms, and I could see how the Lord had directed during the four years our family lived in Oklahoma. We then committed to hold a meeting in Tucson, Arizona—our first meeting as an evangelistic team outside our state. As technology improved, I had upgraded our equipment, and the presentations were becoming smoother. I was excited over the possibilities of presenting the gospel in such an easy-to-understand fashion.

Pants on fire

Our team rented apartments adjacent to each other in Tucson, not far from the meeting site. Marilyn was not feeling well, so it was good to have Melvin and Allene right next door, especially since Marilyn and Allene had known each other since childhood.

The little decks off the back of our apartments intrigued Jimmy, especially where a concrete wall separated the two living spaces, and being almost eleven years old, he had become quite fascinated with matches.

"Son, I don't want you playing with matches. They're dangerous until you're older and know what you're doing," I had said several times. But boys will be boys.

In a couple of days, he decided to pay a visit, next door, via the back deck. Being quite athletic, he began to pull himself over the high concrete wall, dragging and pulling his lower body behind him. Suddenly, the forbidden matches in his pocket ignited from scraping against the concrete!

"Help! My pants are on fire!" he screamed, and before his flaming pants could be removed, Jimmy suffered a painful second-degree burn on his leg. Our adventuresome boy learned a hard lesson in obedience.

But a more ominous shadow loomed over our family.

Chapter 15

"I'll Meet You in Heaven"

"He who loses his life for My sake will find it."
—Matthew 10:39, NKJV

Laura had been begging to attend boarding school. Her aunt, Charlene, who was six weeks younger, planned to attend Ozark Academy in Arkansas for her sophomore year, but Laura decided she wanted to go to Highland Academy in Tennessee, instead.

"But Laura, wouldn't you rather be at home one more year before going away to school?" Marilyn asked.

"Oh, Mom, I love it at home, of course," she replied with fifteen-year-old tact, "but with all the traveling you and Dad must do, it just seems like it would be easier on everyone—especially me—to have a 'normal' school year. And since Charlene is going away . . ."

Marilyn smiled. It hadn't been that long since she was young herself, and even though Laura looked a lot like her, she had her dad's independent spirit. It was hard for Marilyn to think of giving up her daughter a year sooner than she had planned, but no one worked harder than she did to make Laura's dream happen.

School clothes were purchased or made, along with curtains, a bedspread, linens, an iron, toiletries, and all that a girl needs to transition from home to dorm life. It was an exciting day for Laura, and a sad day for Marilyn, when they arrived on the Tennessee boarding school campus. My wife determined that her daughter would not know of her own heavy heart, so she laughed and giggled with her as they hung curtains, filled drawers and closet space, placed towels, and hung pictures.

"Goodbye, my precious!" Marilyn said, as she hugged our daughter, holding back the tears.

"Bye, Mom. Thanks for making everything so nice. I'll write often. Promise!"

Marilyn smiled bravely and quickly got into the car, waving as she drove away. She hoped Laura hadn't seen her tears.

A very ill lady

Marilyn's health was definitely deteriorating. As the Tucson meetings began, she was tiring rapidly and having difficulty breathing. Though she was my greatest supporter and helper, I insisted she drop everything and rest. That didn't seem to help, and one day she was so weak I had to take her to the hospital. As her condition grew steadily worse, her doctor expressed grave concern.

"Mrs. Cox, you are a very ill lady," the heart specialist warned. "You must have that mitral valve replaced as soon as possible because it's threatening your life."

"Yes, I understand," she said weakly, "but we actually live in Oklahoma City, so I need to get back there to have the surgery. The problem is, due to my husband's work, we can't possibly leave here before December 5."

"Then we're going to try to get as much fluid as possible off your lungs and see if we can get you in traveling condition," he said. "I can release you only if you will not exert yourself at all—not one bit of packing, no stresses whatsoever. You must remain right here in this bed until the car is loaded, and then absolutely relax on the trip back to Oklahoma. I will make the arrangements for you at the Presbyterian Hospital in Oklahoma City, and when you arrive, you must check in immediately. I cannot emphasize how ill you are. You will only grow weaker and weaker until that heart valve is replaced."

Love letters to a daughter

Laura, away at boarding school, received the following letter from her mom.

> Tucson Medical Center
> November 30, 1973
>
> Dear Laura,
> Just a note to say I'm thinking of you. I'd like to just pick up the phone and call. All the fluid is off my lungs and my heart is doing much better. Guess I definitely need the mitral valve replaced, so I don't really know what this next month holds.
> Tonight is Friday night and my roommate has the TV going, but thought I would write you a note. I've gotten so many flowers; you'd almost think it was a funeral here! People have been so thoughtful. They seem like old friends that we met in college or maybe even relatives.
> Well, I got this far earlier and then started having company. Must have been eight or ten people came by. Betty is truly a converted Baptist turned Seventh-day Adventist. She loves to talk, like Rosie. She and her husband were baptized last Sabbath. She has really accepted the Lord with all her heart. She's actually more like a sister to me. We talked about everything from soup to nuts. I hope you can meet her. Daddy's plane is due in any time now.
> Not much more news. Let us hear from you soon. We love you lots.
> As always,
> Mother

As soon as the meetings were over, Jimmy and I finished packing our family's things into the car, and we all headed for Oklahoma.

Once we arrived, however, Marilyn insisted on washing all our clothes before going to the hospital. True to his word, the doctor in Tucson had made all the arrangements for Marilyn's transfer, and she was admitted to the Presbyterian Hospital.

Her heart specialist explained that artificial mitral valves last only between twelve and fifteen years. It had been thirteen years since Marilyn's previous surgery, and that's why she was becoming weak and having difficulty breathing. Now, in spite of the fact that she'd almost died during her earlier surgery, Marilyn was faced with open-heart surgery again—and it must be done soon. The surgery was scheduled for Monday, December 18, 1973. Again she wrote to Laura:

Sunday, December 10

Dear Laura,

Well, it's eight days before my surgery, and thought I'd give you a brief report. Sure enough, here I am in the hospital in Oklahoma City! Most everything is done at home except for ironing Dad's shirts. Maxine or Margaret [Marilyn's sisters] would iron them if he would ask them. Both he and Jimmy will have clean clothes anyway.

Laura, I'm so sorry to think of you coming home to a sick mom with no preparation for Christmas. Most of all, I hope you'll be able to get some rest. Daddy has been so sweet and thoughtful. And so has Jimmy. I'm sure you and Charlene can both spend some time shopping once you get home.

We just received your school bill, and I want to tell you how much we appreciate all your hard work. You've done very well at paying your bill. I hope you study hard and make good grades. God will help you remember what you have studied as you take your exams.

I got a letter from Lyle and Rosie. They are moving to Ontario, Kansas. Rosie just had surgery.

We've had more people at the meetings than usual. Melvin and Allene are supposed to be here tomorrow. Daddy has been making up some graphs and charts that are very interesting. I'm anxious to see what comes of their meeting Wednesday morning.

We'll probably talk to you by the time you get this letter. But, Laura, just in case something should go wrong here, I want you to know that I'll meet you in heaven.

Good night—God bless you.

Love,

Mother

A hundred thousand questions

Laura flew home from Nashville on Sunday evening, December 17, a day before Marilyn's surgery, but her flight was late, and her luggage wasn't on her flight. When we finally left the airport, we headed straight for the hospital. Marilyn was delighted to see us all.

"It's so good to have our family all together," she said, smiling.

It was late, and our visit was all too brief, but we returned early the next day before her surgery. We prayed together and felt the usual jitters connected with a hospital procedure—especially one so potentially serious. Before she was wheeled out of the room, my wife turned to me.

"Ken, I want you to know that I love you with all my heart—even if it's not very good." Tearfully, I smiled and squeezed her hand.

My mother-in-law and I took turns pacing the waiting room. Finally, the heart surgeon came out and said, "Mr. Cox, your wife's surgery was successful." Then he paused, as if to say more, but changed his mind.

"When will I be able to see her, doctor?"

The surgeon patted my shoulder but left without a word.

"What did that mean?" my mother-in-law asked.

"I don't know, but something doesn't seem quite right," I answered.

The doctor was in and out of her room in intensive care many times that first night. Finally, he told me he was afraid something might have gone wrong with the anesthesia and that he didn't want to leave until he knew she would wake up.

But Marilyn didn't wake up for two days, and the doctor had to care for other patients. She didn't seem to move at all, but I continued to believe she would soon be conscious. On the third day I was standing by her bed when she opened her eyes. Then she lapsed into unconsciousness again, and seemed to quit breathing. I realized something was tragically wrong, so I quickly pressed the call button for the nurse.

"May I help you?"

"Yes! I think my wife is dying. Help! Quick!"

Immediately, hospital personnel flooded her cubicle. I didn't understand what was going on, but a doctor pushed past me and told me to leave the room. When I was allowed to return about thirty minutes later, Marilyn had a tracheal tube down her throat. Though her eyes were still closed, at least she was breathing. Although I asked the doctors repeatedly, they never explained her condition.

Days passed, and Christmas was forgotten that year, though grandparents and relatives tried to bring some normalcy and cheer to Jimmy and Laura. When it was time for school in January, Laura enrolled in the local ten-grade academy for the rest of the year so she could be near her mother and help with homemaking responsibilities. I'm sure they felt stretched beyond their tender years. Jimmy also returned to school, but we all felt dazed. The children stopped at the hospital every day after school, and I took them home every night after my evening visit. Meanwhile, Marilyn lay in intensive care for three weeks without moving. Several times her heart stopped beating, but each time she was revived.

Eventually, Marilyn was moved to a private room. Some days she was conscious and would mouth words to the children, but the way her words were put together didn't always make sense. She said we would try to get "a puppy poodle" for Jimmy soon, but other days she didn't respond to the children's presence at all.

In mid-January, the doctors decided to take her off the heart monitor, and again I pled with the Lord all night to heal my wife. My children desperately need their mother, Lord, and oh, how I need my wife!

On January 17, I was beside her bed when her eyes opened, and she appeared to rally.

"What have they done to me, Ken?"

As I began to explain what I understood about her condition, Marilyn's eyes closed, and she made no further response. When visiting hours were over, I sadly left for home. Late that night my phone rang, and I left for the hospital without telling the children where I was going. Hours later I returned through fog so thick, I had to lower the driver's window and hold my head out to find the center line.

I went straight to Laura's room, and my eyes must have told her the sad news before I could speak. Then we both went to Jimmy's room and awakened him. Though the news was almost expected, and certainly feared, it was devastating. Their dearly loved mother was dead at the age of thirty-eight.

I sat on the bed with my arms around them both, and we all cried until we simply couldn't cry anymore.

Why didn't God answer my prayers? Why? A hundred thousand questions filled my mind. What will we do now? Who will help me with the domestic duties and raising the children?

Marilyn was an incredible mother and a devoted wife who cared more for the children and me than anyone else ever could. Not only had she brought fun and laughter to our home, she had loved, encouraged, and helped me in every way. How can I—how can our children—ever manage without her? I wrestled with those questions for weeks until I finally accepted the fact that I was not going to know the answers here on this old earth.

Feeling alone

The day of Marilyn's funeral was the saddest day of our lives. We remembered her beautiful, selfless life, but knew she was gone from us for the rest of our earthly days. Teary-eyed church and family members expressed their love and concern in many thoughtful ways, but no amount of sympathy could take away the ache of our loss.

My sixteen-year-old daughter and eleven-year-old son went home with me that night after committing their mother's body to the earth—realizing that life would never, ever, be the same again. We were filled with so much hurt that it was often hard to breathe. Stunned and reeling myself, I only vaguely sensed my children's deep, traumatic loss. It was too much for my mind to comprehend. One lonely day followed another, and our family didn't feel like a family anymore. The most important person in our world—the one who held us all together, who loved and nurtured and cared for each of us—was gone.

Marilyn's parents and sisters brought food, invited us over, and tried to help in every way, even as they grieved the loss of their beloved daughter and sister. Though their expressions of love and concern were much appreciated, we simply hurt too much to be consoled.

When the autopsy report finally came, it indicated that Marilyn had not received sufficient oxygen during surgery, resulting in her untimely death. But what could be done to rectify that now?

The children returned to school, but coming home was a painful daily duty. In addition to their heavy school load, Laura and Jimmy tried to keep up with all the household chores their mother used to accomplish so easily. It was frustrating and nearly more than they could handle. I had no heart for much of anything, but continued to study and prepare my sermons. Though the children and I were together, we each felt alone. Something—someone—at our core was missing.

Gradually, I began to realize that I must accept anew my most basic beliefs by faith: that God had loved Marilyn, God loved me, and

God loved my children. It didn't mean we wouldn't have pain. No, we were going to hurt deeply and greatly miss Marilyn, but by faith I knew we would see her again someday.

Chapter 16

Tried by Fire

Though he slay me, yet will I trust in him.
—Job 13:15, KJV

Kimber Johnson, president of the Kentucky-Tennessee Conference of Seventh-day Adventists, extended an invitation for me to become their conference evangelist. Because I'd covered most of the state of Oklahoma already, and because my dear wife was now sleeping in Jesus, it seemed the right time to make a move. Perhaps we could better begin a new life without Marilyn in a location without sad memories. Before the end of February, Nashville, Tennessee, had become our new home.

But Laura opted to stay with her grandparents and attend Ozark Academy with Charlene, while Jim accepted an invitation to remain with Uncle Jerry and Aunt Martha in Oklahoma until the school year closed.

My first evangelistic meetings began in mid-March in Paducah, Kentucky. A young couple came the second night and took their places near the front of the auditorium. Sandy Powell was a Seventh-day Adventist, but her husband, Lin, had quit attending because he felt that he was not good enough to be counted with "the saints."

The Powells owned a battery distribution business in Paducah, and Lin enjoyed traveling. That was fortunate, for his work required a lot of it! However, somehow, between his wife and the Holy Spirit, his schedule allowed him a couple of days at home right after our series began. Later, he said that when he attended that first meeting, he knew the Lord had opened a way for him to come back to Christ.

Lin cleared his schedule of all travel for the remainder of the series. And when an altar call was made, he requested to be the first one in the baptistry—whenever the time for baptisms came—"Because I'm the chief of sinners," he explained. From that point on, if I was holding a series of meetings within driving distance, Sandy and Lin were there for at least three evening meetings every weekend.

So passionate was their desire to serve the Lord that after they had volunteered for several months, I asked Lin if he would like to lead out in my "Operation Andrew" plan, which followed the example of the apostle Andrew in teaching church members how to bring their brothers to Christ. Lin was enthusiastic about this and felt that with his business degree and experience, he and Sandy could develop it even further. For a while they continued running their business along with working in our ministry, but eventually they sold their business and worked full time for the Lord.

Married again

I had been in the Kentucky-Tennessee Conference for only a short while when I was advised, "You need to get married. It's not good for an evangelist as young as you are to be single and traveling all over the conference. People will talk."

I hadn't even considered such a thing. I had just wanted to bury myself in my work to forget the haunting loneliness. But maybe there was something to the advice. I didn't want to bring discredit to the Lord's work, and when I allowed myself to think about it, I admitted that I was lonely—painfully so. No one could ever take Marilyn's place, but I decided to pray about the possibility of remarrying.

During a series of meetings in Nashville, Tennessee, a woman approached me and said, "Saturday night we're going to have a party, and we'd like for you to come."

I hesitated momentarily, and then answered, "Well, *hmm,* sure, I'd like to do that." But as I did a bit of checking on the "party," I discovered that I seemed to be the only male attending while seven women were invited! *Hmmm.*

This was too uncomfortable, so I called my friends, Sam and Valda Martz, and explained the situation.

"Listen," I said, "you've got to get me out of this!"

They agreed to handle it, and I was released from my "party" obligation!

After a couple of other potentially embarrassing situations, the advice of the "brethren" began to make more sense. I had heard a former classmate from Keene was now a widow. Because her husband had also been a classmate, surely we already had a lot in common. Before the summer ended, we found ourselves in a whirlwind courtship—mostly by telephone.

Maurita was the daughter of missionaries, attractive, and liked to sing, and it seemed like a wonderful mix. She also had two boys, ages fifteen and ten, and we hit it off immediately.

We spent hours on the phone together. Maybe, just maybe, we could find happiness again—together. Marilyn had always managed the home front so well, and I knew I needed help on that score. Regrettably, I'd been mostly an absentee dad during the children's early years, and now I certainly was floundering in my attempt to fill the roles of both mother and father to them. What should I do?

I reasoned that it would be good for them to have a mother figure back in their lives. Yes, it might be a way to give them roots. As much as I was away, having someone at home to love and care for Jimmy would be stabilizing for him. And Laura, even though she was at school, needed a mother. And, yes, it would be great to be warmly welcomed home myself after a busy series of meetings!

Maurita and I were married in December 1974.

Miraculous healing

Almost any evangelist will tell you that more things go wrong when a sermon on the mark of the beast is preached than on any other subject. It came up during a program at a high school auditorium in Louisville, Kentucky, one evening. Though it had been storming and pouring rain, a crowd had come out anyway because of the intriguing subject, and the auditorium was full.

While I was engrossed in my sermon, water began oozing under the doors. Soon streams of water were pouring in, and in a matter of minutes, the floor was covered! I had to dismiss the meeting quickly, and people had to wade to their cars. By the time we turned off all the equipment and had taken everything down, we had to wade through water up to our waists to get to our cars! Fortunately, the parking lot was on higher ground.

By the next meeting, everything had dried out, and several days later, a young girl who appeared to be about twelve years old came up to me.

"Pastor Cox, would you pray for me?"

"Why, of course, I will pray for you," I answered. "Is there something in particular you want me to pray about?"

"I've got something wrong with my kidneys, and I could die from it. When the meetings are over, Mom and Dad are taking me to the Mayo Clinic for tests. So would you pray for me, please?"

"I'd be honored to pray for you, but why don't we do it like the Bible says? I'll get some of the other pastors together, and we'll all pray for you and anoint you with oil, just like it says in James."

After the service that evening, we prayed and anointed that girl according to Scripture.

"Be strong in your faith," I told her. "God loves you, and He will hear and answer your prayers."

Her parents took her to the Mayo Clinic after the meetings were over, where they ran tests for two days. On the third day, the doctor called in her parents.

"We cannot find any signs of a kidney problem in your daughter," he said.

"Fine!" her mother said, relieved. "We'll just take her home."

"But we know from all the records you brought that there is a problem," the doctor insisted. "In fact, the paperwork even shows where they did surgery. But we can't find signs of that surgery! Let's keep her here a few more days and run some more tests, just to be sure."

She stayed a few more days, but the specialists were never able to find any indication of kidney disease. The Lord had completely healed her—what a miracle!

Why the Lord answers a prayer for healing affirmatively one time and not another is probably far beyond human understanding, since no one can see His overall plan. But He is God, and His children must learn to trust Him, whether shadows flee away or grow deeper and darker. Such trust isn't always easy to maintain.

Stacking the odds

I held meetings in cities across the South for the Southern Union. A new couple, Jim and Corinne Ferguson, joined me, along with Melvin and Allene Weber. Corinne was an organist—in fact, she had played the organ for our meetings in Tulsa—and Jim helped with visitation. With attendance growing larger and larger, the Fergusons were a welcome addition to share in the mounting workload.

Every evening we held a drawing just before the lecture began, and whoever's name was called would receive a very nicely bound religious book or a Bible. One night, as the name was handed to me, I read aloud, "Jimmy Cox." Actually, almost before the words were out of my mouth, I found Jimmy with my eyes.

"Well, he's part of the family, and we don't allow family to participate in the drawing, you know," I stated with a brief smile.

As I asked for another name to be drawn, young Jimmy's return smile changed to a strange look of panic.

"Lanier Ferguson," I read out loud. That was Jim and Corinne Ferguson's son—Jimmy's best friend.

"Sorry, he's part of the family also."

The next name was pulled out, and my eyebrows rose slightly.

"Jimmy Cox! *Hmm*," I mused aloud. "I think Jimmy and I might need

Phil Draper and Allene Weber

to have a little father and son talk after the program tonight!" A titter went through the crowd. The boys had obviously stuffed the drawing box!

Shaken up

Jim and Corinne Ferguson left to pastor a church, and I was in need of someone to play the organ and piano. Allene had met a young man she thought would be a good addition to the team. Phil Draper was a handsome young school teacher with a contagious personality, blond hair, and twinkling eyes. He was also single.

Phil could carry the program with or without written music and always seemed to know just the right song for the occasion—it just flowed from his quick fingers, and he made a strong team member in many ways.

We worked well together, and whenever I would reprogram my slide programs, Phil worked diligently with me for days, usually late into the night. Updating the sermon illustrations was a major undertaking—changing thousands of slides to all new graphics, including pictures, quotations, and Bible texts. Every glass slide had to be carefully cleaned, pictures and other graphics cut a critical way with a difficult machine, and then these had to be carefully mounted—exactly straight. Each slide was then placed into its exact slot in one of hundreds of carousel trays for each multimedia program.

Late one evening in 1975, we were working on a major reprogramming effort in the old Southern Publishing Association building in Nashville, Tennessee. We had disassembled the old materials and were ready to begin the reassembly process. All at once the entire building began to move, and the carousel trays containing the glass-mounted slides began to slide around the tabletops.

"No!" Phil exclaimed, "This can't be an earthquake—not in Tennessee!"

But it was. Fortunately, it was not a severe one. Perhaps God spoke to the earthquake, as He had to the waves long ago, "Peace, be still."

All grown up

As the children grew up, I told them that they didn't have to finish

Left to right: Erica, Roger, Stacy, Laura, and Larry Becker

college, but they had to attend at least three years. The Lord was very good to me and blessed me with good children; and I never had to tell them to study. Laura enrolled at Southern Missionary College, where she received her registered nurse's degree. She met Larry Becker, son of Pastor A. C. and Helen Becker. He was a theology student, a handsome, dedicated young man who never met a stranger. In June of 1979, Laura and Larry were married in a beautiful ceremony in the Ooltewah, Tennessee, Seventh-day Adventist Church with both their fathers participating as ministers. After Larry finished his master's program in theology at Andrews University, Laura completed her

Jim, Taylor, and Shaun Cox

four-year college degree. They began pastoring in the Georgia-Cumberland Conference. They have two children, Roger and Erica.

Jimmy attended Collegedale Academy and graduated from Ozark Academy in Arkansas. But he had a desire to become an attorney. Unfortunately, within the Adventist educational system, there is no program for those who want to study law. Because of the ties Jimmy had with Marilyn's family in Oklahoma, he applied to Oklahoma University, just outside of Oklahoma City, and was accepted. He graduated in 1989 with a degree in law and set up his law practice in Las Vegas, Nevada, where he met Shaun Bruce, a legal secretary. They have a daughter, Taylor.

"Get up! Get out!"

Team members become like family, but things have a way of quickly changing, and when Melvin Weber got word that a company he had invested in was going through a severe crisis, he had to step out of his evangelism coordinator role and take over management of the company. Both he and Allene had given faithful service, and I missed them. Fortunately, the Lord provided, and Lin Powell was able to step into Melvin's role, in addition to his Operation Andrew functions. But we were still short-handed, both in vocal music and in visitation help.

Sandy and Lin Powell

Benny Moore, a friend of Phil Draper, was an accountant in Chattanooga, Tennessee. Benny agreed to help with both music and visitation. He not only sang well, but also had a good understanding of computers—an ability useful in tracking guests' names and visitation records. With his strong accounting background, Benny used his expertise in streamlining the bookkeeping process and keeping financial records in good order. He was also outgoing and friendly to all.

Benny's wife, Barbara, loved children and immediately sensed a need for a children's program, which she designed and personally conducted during every series for many years. The children's program was also designed to lead children of all ages to Christ. Benny and Barbara were a wonderful addition.

Benny and Barbara Moore

Early in 1976, Phil and I were again gathering material to reprogram slides. We had been to all the publishing houses as well as to the Adventist Media Center in Los Angeles. At the Breath of Life headquarters, we were able to photograph illustrations featuring African American subjects.

The next day we planned to catch an early flight to Mountain View, California, where we would complete our photo collection at Pacific Press®. Maurita and I had a room just down the hall from Phil on the first floor of the Ramada Inn, near the Los Angeles International Airport. Phil was sound asleep around 2:00 A.M. when someone banged on his door and yelled, "Fire!"

Jumping out of bed, dazed and wondering if he'd had a nightmare, Phil ran to his door and threw it open. Sure enough, the hall was ablaze! Smoke billowed everywhere, and the top half of his room door was already charred and burning.

"Help!" he yelled, thinking someone was there to lead him to safety. "Help!" But no one answered.

In his panic, he'd forgotten that he was on the first floor and could have gone out the window, but he did realize that he must get to us and get out. Crouching low, he ran down the burning, smoke-filled hallway and banged on our door.

"Get up! Get out!" Phil yelled. "The hotel is on fire!"

I opened the door slightly, saw the fire, and slammed it shut. Maurita and I quickly gathered up our things, while Phil ran outside to the pool area, picked up a chair, and broke out our window.

"Come, Maurita!" Phil cried urgently.

Trembling, she was soon out the window, after passing her luggage out first. Then Phil and I, adrenaline pumping, remembered all the expensive Hasselblad professional camera equipment in the room. Amazingly, we managed to get almost everything out, including my suitcase.

Not knowing what else to do, the three of us headed for the lobby. Fire trucks and emergency personnel were swarming, and hotel guests were screaming and jumping off balconies in every stage of undress. Unfortunately, that night the entire hotel went up in flames, and two people perished. It made Maurita's loss of her watch and Phil's loss of his clothing and suitcases seem like nothing.

The Ramada put all their frightened clients on buses and took them to another Ramada Inn not far from the airport. We were given rooms—on the eleventh floor. However, none of us could sleep that far above ground level that night—or for years to come!

The next day, after filing insurance claims for our lost belongings, we headed on to Pacific Press® where, though shaken, we completed gathering the pictures we needed.

Irreconcilable differences

Our marriage was slowly deteriorating. Maurita and I both had hoped our new mate would fill the aching emptiness left from the loss of our deceased spouses. But alas, what our marriage brought instead was bitter disappointment for both parties almost from the first, and eventually, it crumbled into disaster. Blending our lives seemed fraught with insurmountable challenges and enormous frustrations. We spent time in counseling and devoted much sincere effort in trying to work out our differences. Finally, we determined that it would be best for each of us to go our separate ways. "Irreconcilable differences," the court called it.

Left to right: Bob, Tammy, Matthew, and Luke Vaughn

Left to right: Jillian, Bart, Linda, and Jimmy Vaughan

But one good thing came out of that union—a wonderful relationship with Maurita's two sons, Bart and Bob. They have since grown up to be fine Christian young men with families of their own. Bart graduated from La Sierra College with a degree in landscaping and did upper division work at California Polytech State University in horticulture. He married Linda Anderson, and they have two children, Jillian and Jimmy. Bob graduated from Loma Linda University with a degree in medicine, married Tammy Ellis, and they have two boys, Matt and Luke. I consider these children my grandchildren. We have had the opportunity to spend many happy hours together.

Unfortunately, this failed marriage left a dark cloud over my ministry and me. I was sorely discouraged over its failure for a long, long time.

An "evangelistic" wedding

Pastor Bob Everett invited us to hold a series of meetings in Des Moines, Iowa, outside of the Kentucky-Tennessee Conference. A bright and lovely young woman named Joey Chapman came to the meetings, and someone whispered to us that she had a lovely singing voice. Of course, Phil accompanied her on the organ. Was it love at first sight? It certainly appeared that way, since the vocalist and the organist were exchanging far more glances than required to perform the music! I invited Joey to sing for our next series, and the romance of the musicians continued to blossom.

Phil and Joey Draper

141

A few months later at a meeting in Charlotte, North Carolina, Phil proposed, and they decided to have their wedding on the last night of that series. The church was packed, and the lights were dimmed. The organist played the wedding march, and greeters came up the aisle as bridesmaids. Then, into the spotlight walked Joey, a strikingly beautiful bride. The congregation seemed to feel honored to participate in the festive occasion.

Sandy and Lin Powell were invited by the Kentucky-Tennessee Conference to work full time for the Lord with their own evangelistic team. After our evangelistic series in Haiti (described in a later chapter), we sadly parted company with our friends. Phil and Joey Draper and Benny and Barbara Moore would now be our core team for the next ten years. I realized I had almost nothing to do with putting that wonderful team together. The Lord's guiding hand had led and opened doors, and I had the privilege of walking through them.

Chapter 17

Kodak: Special Delivery

*"You will find your joy in the Lord, and I will
cause you to ride on the heights of the land."*
—Isaiah 58:14, NIV

Dr. Russell Long and his wife, Lucile, from the Charlotte Adventist church, invited our team to visit Haiti to see the mission project they were involved in. This resulted in an invitation from the Haitian mission to hold meetings in Port-au-Prince, the capital city.

There we faced electrical problems we hadn't encountered before. Electricity in the United States is 60 cycles, but in Haiti it's 50 cycles. Kodak had just announced that they were coming out with a new slide projector that would automatically adjust from one cycle to the other as well as from 110 to 220 voltage. This feature would allow us to purchase new projectors that could be used not only in Haiti, but also all over the world. With all the new technological advances of the 1970s, we were now using one large screen with twenty-one projectors. So I ordered twenty-five of these new projectors to be delivered three months before the meetings were to begin.

The delivery date came and went, but no projectors arrived. "Mr. Cox," the salesman explained over the phone, "we've had a glitch in the production of the projectors. But don't worry. We'll have them to you in plenty of time."

Another month passed. Still no projectors. "Mr. Cox, the problem is almost solved, and we'll be shipping them all to you in the next few days."

Another month passed. Still no projectors! We received promises, but nothing more. Finally, two weeks before departure, I called Kodak in desperation and asked to speak to the president.

The woman who answered the phone said, "I'm so sorry, Mr. Cox. The president is in a board meeting right now. Is there anyone else who could help you?"

"If you have someone capable of making decisions and getting it done, I'd like to talk to that person," I responded.

In just a moment, a man's voice came over the phone, "Can I help you?"

"Well, yes, if you can get something done," I said.

"I guess it would be pretty sad if I couldn't because I'm chairman of the board," the man answered.

I explained my problem again, this time with renewed hope.

"Mr. Cox," he answered, "you will have your projectors if I have to bring them to you myself."

In two days, twenty-five projectors were sitting on my doorstep. However, once we got to Haiti and began using them, we had a serious problem. The flow of electricity was undependable, and sometimes the power would spike. When it did, it would often blow a fuse deep inside a projector. There was no way to replace it, even if we'd had a fuse, because it was impossible for us to open the machine.

Once again I called Kodak—from Haiti.

"Put the projector on a plane, and we'll send you a new projector to replace it," was the answer.

Over the next few weeks, fuses blew in at least half a dozen projectors. In each case we sent them by plane to Kodak, and the next day we'd receive a free replacement. I was happy I had several spare projectors, but Kodak never failed to respond to our needs, and I was grateful they were such a responsible company.

The market

Unaccustomed to traveling outside the United States, our team was fascinated by everything in Haiti—the people with their warm hearts and dazzling smiles, the abundance of tropical flowers, breadfruit hanging in massive green trees—and, of course, the most impossible traffic jams! But what fascinated us the most were the sights and smells of the market. Seemingly every tropical fruit grows abundantly in Haiti, along with delectable fresh vegetables.

Barbara Lonstrom was a masterful bargainer. With great animation she would haggle with vendors, eventually returning to the van with a dozen large avocados that she had purchased for one American dollar. Artwork, wood carvings, and other souvenirs were plentiful and reasonable.

Our team members were truly "innocents abroad" and approached their assignments with eagerness and enthusiasm, knowing no fear or limitations. The sky was the limit in this incredibly beautiful mission field so close to home.

Sometimes we took advantage of our free mornings (our only free time) for a quick tour of the countryside, or we'd go to the ocean for snorkeling. Barbara and her cook provided a lunch entrée for us every day, and we purchased vegetables and fruit to round out the meal. Each food item was washed in a solution containing both soap and bleach to kill any bacteria that could have made us sick.

Delightful problems

After lunch, our team dressed for the evening meeting and walked through the streets of the capital toward the auditorium, where we stayed late each evening. Several Haitian children eagerly volunteered to help us with every imaginable chore—nothing was beneath them. We grew to know and love some of our young helpers especially well, and our hearts were moved to help these youth with their education.

Poverty in Haiti is unlike anything most Americans have ever seen. It is depressing, overpowering, and all-pervasive. But money is not the answer for the Haitian's problems. The only relief from such grinding poverty and unsanitary conditions will be the coming of Jesus Christ.

We did our best to reach as many as possible with His great gospel of love.

But projectors and poverty were not the only challenges we had in Haiti. Some problems were actually delightful. More church members wanted to help with the meetings than we could possibly use, and more people wanted to attend more than the three nightly sessions—for twenty-eight days—than the auditorium could accommodate. When the guards opened the front gates the first evening, two thousand people rushed inside, almost in a stampede, before the gates clanged shut behind them. Nervous team members wondered if the crowd would stop before trampling the screens—and all of us! Benches designed to hold ten often held twenty as people squeezed together to maximize the space allowed so everyone could "see the show."

Five giant screens were erected up front, and the fifth, containing text printed in French, helped them understand the message more easily. This being our first international crusade, we had worked diligently to get the slides translated properly.

The scene was repeated evening after evening, meeting after meeting. Guards opened the gates; two thousand people rushed in; guards quickly closed the gates. When that meeting ended, people left through another exit, and within minutes, another two thousand would rush in.

The hall was two blocks from the presidential palace, and the Haitian church members made determined efforts to reach and invite the country's educated people. Approximately three hundred teachers, businessmen, and government officials filled reserved seats each evening.

In addition to our team, twenty-six pastors of the South Haitian Mission, fifteen senior theology students from Port-au-Prince Adventist Seminary, and more than 250 church members helped in the evangelistic series. Guy Valleray, ministerial secretary of the Franco-Haitian Union, translated my sermons into French.

With such an exhausting schedule, we were all amazed how God strengthened us so that we never lost our voices or our enthusiasm. The generous and eager Haitian people energized us all. It was a taste of what evangelism would be like in the rest of the Inter-American Division, where we spent the next couple of years.

Eventually, more than seven hundred people were baptized in the beautiful Caribbean Sea because of the Holy Spirit's work. Several hundred more continued to study and were baptized later. Everywhere, God guides men and women who have deep yearnings to hear the story of salvation. What a thrill to heed Jesus' final instructions to His disciples "that repentance and remission of sins should be preached in his name among all nations" (Luke 24:47, KJV).

Chapter 18

About My Father's Business

*"Your light will rise in the darkness, and your
night will become like the noonday."*
—Isaiah 58:10, NIV

Shortly after the faith venture to Haiti, our team was invited to spend two years working for the Inter-American Division, its territory stretches from Mexico through Central America and the Caribbean Islands to Venezuela and Colombia. Ben Archibald—a dynamic leader, and a kind and benevolent man—was the division president. His vision for "sowing the field" became apparent when he invited me to attend a division meeting. As I looked over the agenda, I noticed that the first item of business was evangelism.

After the meeting, I asked Ben about it.

"We always put evangelism at the top," he answered, "and when we get that taken care of, we go on to the other items. If you want your churches to grow, you need to do evangelism; if you want the church schools to grow, do evangelism; if you want the publishing houses to grow, do evangelism. It's just a matter of keeping our priorities straight."

Perhaps that's why membership in the Inter-American Division has grown exponentially!

So our team moved to this new mission field—and into the most exciting two-year period of our lives. We moved our offices to Coral Gables, Florida, even though most of us had homes in Collegedale, Tennessee.

We held organizational meetings with local pastors, and department heads were selected to help run each series throughout the division. They all chose to conduct meetings seven nights a week, with three back-to-back sessions each day—just as we had done in Haiti.

Sixty-seven weddings

Guatemala City, Guatemala, was the site of our first meeting. Some team members drove their fifth-wheel trailers down through Mexico and parked near the meeting place. Because no available auditorium was large enough to accommodate the crowds, the conference had purchased a huge circus tent, which they called *la carpa gigante* (the giant tent). It was truly a monster. With seating capacity for more than two thousand, it had to be erected on a large vacant lot on the edge of the city. Pastors came in droves to help put up this huge canvas structure, and tropical rains didn't make the job any easier. But eventually the poles were in place, the ropes stretched to their limits, and the chairs arranged inside.

Thousands of people came to the meetings and made decisions to follow Christ. But some unique problems surfaced. Many couples had separated from their first spouses and had been living for years with another partner, producing children from the new union. Their former spouses had done the same thing. Because of the strong Roman Catholic influence in the area, these people were denied the possibility of divorce or remarriage. After attending the meetings and learning the truths of God's Word, they desired to become members of the Seventh-day Adventist Church. So one evening, we conducted a large marriage ceremony involving sixty-seven couples; the next day they followed the Lord in baptism.

Immediately, a new church sprang up in Guatemala City, a direct result of the Holy Spirit's powerful moving.

Held at gunpoint

Our next series was in Panama City, Panama. What a challenge it was to maneuver our RVs down the Pan-American Highway! Everywhere we stopped, curious eyes peered through the windows. Americans in rolling metal homes were a real curiosity.

At the border of Nicaragua, getting through customs seemed to take an interminably long time. Because they happened to be closed for the day when we arrived, it was considered necessary in this unsettled Communist country to hold us—at gunpoint—until the next morning, when we were ultimately pronounced safe for passage.

The Panama meetings were held in a brand-new convention center on the shore of the Pacific Ocean. In this large auditorium that seated thousands, we put up a twelve- by forty-eight-foot screen with twenty-one projectors so the people could see even from the back of the auditorium.

When moving from country to country to hold meetings, we always faced the potential problem of the current not matching the equipment; but in this case, the auditorium wiring had been improperly installed. When we plugged in our equipment, twelve projectors instantly burned up. How could we open with only half of our equipment?

For the first few nights, each team member was assigned to three projectors. Because the slides had to be rearranged, our sequence was off, and each team member had to manually change the slides. But without question, God answered our prayers. The team members knew the program so well that they were able to make the changes with few problems while waiting for the new projectors to arrive.

A new church was erected in Panama City under the sweet influence of God's Holy Spirit. They named it the Dimensiones Proféticas church, after our Dimensions of Prophecy series.

A total change of life

During the Panama City meetings, we saw a remarkable miracle revealing God's power. A man came to me about two weeks into the meetings saying that this was the first time he had attended religious meetings, and as he learned more and more, his conviction had grown that he needed to accept Christ. But he had a problem. He now understood that living a homosexual lifestyle was wrong, but he had been gay as long as he could remember, and he didn't know how to change.

I shared with him Scripture passages showing that God considers homosexual practices to be sinful. "God is more than capable of changing our desires and way of life if we will accept Him and allow Him to guide and control us," I assured him.

Right there in the auditorium, he expressed an earnest desire to follow God in every aspect of his life. "But," he said, "I'm concerned that after you leave the country, I might fall back into my old ways."

So I went to the local pastor and asked if he would be willing to give this man some pastoral help. "If you can visit with him," I said, "and support him spiritually for a few weeks, I believe his commitment to Christ will prove genuine." I didn't tell him what the man's problem was.

A couple of days later, shortly after he had met the new convert, the pastor came back to me. He was concerned that because their backgrounds were so vastly different, they wouldn't relate well to each other. As I spoke with him, I realized that my pastor friend was still not aware of the root problem, so I acquainted him with it, and after some encouragement—and the Lord's blessing—he did counsel this man, sharing the power of the gospel. Over the next few weeks, the Holy Spirit took over and totally changed the man's heart! The last I heard, he was happily married with a lovely family—and continues to love God sincerely.

Lost freight

While preparing for departure to Trinidad, we were told that two of our pieces—the organ and the generator—were too large to check as excess baggage. Both would have to go as freight. We were concerned whether they would get to our site on time, so we negotiated with the freight handlers to put the two items on the same plane we were on. Now the problem was that we had to change planes in Jamaica. When we landed and asked about our organ and generator, the freight employee replied that the items must go to their warehouse before being sent on to Trinidad.

During our layover in Jamaica, we decided to go to the warehouse ourselves and see if we could get the shipment expedited. We were astonished by the warehouse's size—a block square and thirty feet high. Freight was stacked to the ceiling, with an occasional aisle separating the mountains of freight.

I approached the man who seemed to be in charge. "We have a couple of pieces of freight that just came off the plane, and we'd like to be sure they get air-freighted to Trinidad today. Could you please tell us where they might be?"

"Well, they're here in the warehouse somewhere," he answered simply, "but it would be impossible to get them on a plane going out today."

"If we could find them, would you put them on the plane for us?"

"We don't have any idea where your freight is," he explained. "I'm sure it's buried somewhere in all this other freight, but you could never find it in time to get it on the next plane out."

With that challenge, Benny started off down one aisle and Phil down another. I took a third one. Amazingly, in a matter of minutes, Benny had found the generator perched atop a stack of freight. Shortly thereafter, Phil located the organ.

The men in the freight office promised to put the two items on the plane, and true to their word, when our plane took off, all our luggage—and air freight—was on its way to Trinidad with us.

Getting mountains of equipment from country to country presented some definite challenges. When flying, we always took our equipment as excess baggage, and many times we would arrive at an airport with a hundred boxes. Delta Air Lines finally requested advance notice when we would be traveling with them so they could have extra personnel in place to handle all the additional baggage. Through the blessing of God, we traveled for two years throughout the Inter-American Division without losing a single piece of luggage or freight.

Demon possessed

While I was preaching one evening at the Trinidad meetings, a woman in the congregation stood to her feet and started screaming! The deacons quietly moved toward her, but before they reached her, she passed out and fell into the aisle. They carried her off to another area and prayed earnestly for her. Later that evening, she returned to the crowded auditorium, sitting in the back. Though she now had my attention, and my eyes seemed to follow her every movement, she made no further disturbance. She continued coming to the meetings, and under the Holy Spirit's influence, requested baptism, desiring to fully follow her new Lord. Praise His name!

Another woman who attended our meetings had been jilted when she was young. It seemed that her mind had been affected and she was, even at that point, quite unstable. She came to me and said, "Brother Cox, I want to say something to the audience."

I said, "I'm sorry, but we don't do that."

However, one night while I was speaking, she started forward, obviously intent on interrupting the message. From his perch on the organ bench, Phil could see what was happening and whispered to Benny, "Stop that lady!" Benny rushed over to gently guide the woman offstage. It wasn't as easy as he had hoped, however, and somehow instead of turning her shoulders in another direction, he found his hands unexpectedly around her neck! She cried out, "You don't have to choke me!"

Benny turned red, the congregation smiled, and the Holy Spirit brought us right back to the subject of the evening.

Charles and Ellen Klinke

Afraid for my life

The city of Bogotá, Colombia, was another evangelistic location. Local self-supporting missionaries Charles and Ellen Klinke and their sons, Chip and Willie, were a great help during the meetings. Charlie is a very personable man who easily talks and visits with people. Ellen is extremely organized and capable in directing committee meetings and working with all types of personalities. Every evangelistic meeting in the Inter-American Division was large, with attendance in the thousands. Bogotá was no exception, and the coliseum we rented was full each evening. Because of the crowds, street vendors immediately set up shop to sell their wares every evening.

The hordes of street children in Bogotá with no homes and no one to care for them saddened us. These children's lives consist of finding enough food to survive and a place to sleep at night. Surprisingly, a great number of them came to our meetings, and many of the older ones were baptized. In fact, the mission had to send in additional pastors to assist in the baptisms.

After concluding the service on closing night, I thanked people for coming, and said Goodbye. Suddenly, and unexpectedly, the crowd rose and rushed toward the platform. Before I knew what was going on, people were grabbing my clothing—pulling, tugging, and pushing from every direction! Few times in my life have I ever been afraid of a crowd, but at that moment I sensed my life was in grave danger. Charles Klinke, with his commanding presence, waded through the crowd in a flash, pulling people out of his way like dolls, until he reached the stage and escorted me off the platform to a place of safety. Thanks again, Charlie!

Meeting a drunk

When we couldn't locate an appropriate building for our meetings in Costa Rica, the conference decided to erect a new metal building, which would later be used as a church. So many people came that many of the younger men sat in the rafters. More than any other country we worked in, the Holy Spirit drew teachers, businessmen, lawyers, doctors, and other professionals to those meetings. But not all who came were so well-educated.

At the close of the meeting one evening, a grandmother approached me in tears. "Would you please pray for my grandson?" she begged. "His wife has left him, and he's lost his family because he's drunk all the time, Pastor. Now it looks like he could even lose his job!"

Of course, I prayed with her for her grandson that evening. A few days later, I was interrupted in a workers' meeting I was having with the pastors.

"A fellow out in the lobby wants to talk to you," someone whispered.

Turning the meeting over to a team member, I went out to see who needed to talk to me so desperately. A young man was waiting outside. He was so drunk he could hardly stand up, and his speech was slurred. In broken English he explained that he had lost his job. I deduced from several things he said that this must be the man I had prayed for.

"Pastor, pray for me," he pleaded.

Several thoughts ran through my mind. *Lord, what do I do with someone so drunk he can hardly stand up? He can't speak plainly, so he probably can't understand anything I say. Should I tell him, "Go home and sober up, and then come back and talk to me when you're sober"?*

But then the impression came, *What is there to lose? Even if he doesn't remember anything I say, what have we lost? Besides, this young man could have everything to gain.*

I invited him to sit down with me, right there in the lobby. In a simple way, I presented to him the good news of God's love, and I explained how to accept Jesus Christ as his Lord and Savior.

Though still drunk, the young man appeared to sincerely give his heart and life to the Lord. I never know how sincere someone under the influence really is, but neither do I presume to limit the power of God.

I didn't see him again until I was going down the line, shaking hands with about five hundred precious people who were waiting to be baptized on the last day of our meetings. There he was—clear-eyed and sober, wearing a bright and grateful smile.

"How are you doing?" I asked.

"Since I gave my heart to the Lord, I haven't had anything to drink," he answered. "I've gotten my job back, my wife and children have come home, and my whole life has changed."

"Praise God!" I said with a smile as I hugged him.

Once again, a new church was established, which they also named the Dimensiones Proféticas church, because of the blessings that God granted to our feeble human efforts.

Tickets to the mark of the beast lecture

During the meetings in Guadeloupe, we were housed in a large mansion overlooking the city. It would have been easy to get used to that lifestyle! Every meeting site in each country seemed to bring new friends, new experiences, new challenges, and new spiritual blessings. Our team experienced a splendid, Christlike camaraderie, not only among ourselves, but also with our newfound brothers and sisters.

Almost all the meetings held throughout Central America and the

Caribbean were in regions with large Roman Catholic populations. Some of the subjects presented required attending several nights in order to build a scriptural background. We didn't want to upset people who were not coming regularly, so we required tickets on the night of the mark of the beast presentation. These were given to the people who had attended each evening. To avoid misunderstandings about a sensitive topic, we didn't allow people without tickets to be admitted.

That night, three Catholic priests in their clerical robes walked through the front entrance. Shocked and surprised, the greeters just stepped back and let them in. Evidently, God in His leading wanted them to hear the subject because they didn't give any trouble and seemed to enjoy the meeting. Many people accepted the Lord in Guadeloupe and were baptized.

Come look at this shark!

We had an interesting experience in Guadeloupe when we took a few hours to go snorkeling off the reef between the beach and a nearby small island. To my surprise, I spotted a dead shark caught in a net below me—an unusual sight this close to land.

At the same time, Benny had finally persuaded Barbara to swim the short distance to the other shore—much against her better judgment. While she was swimming, I surfaced and called out from thirty feet away, "Hey, Benny, when you have a minute, come look at this shark!"

That was all Barbara needed to hear! Forget swimming—period!

She never again set foot in the ocean for the remainder of our tour in this tropical paradise.

Caught in a battle

Our two years with the Inter-American Division ended all too quickly. Our fifth-wheel/motor home convoy began its long trek north, with Phil and Joey in the lead. We were passing through El

Salvador when Phil suddenly stopped his rig ahead of us and just sat there. We stopped also, of course, but wondered why we weren't moving. We had lots of miles to cover!

After a few minutes, I got out of my pickup to find out what was going on. Immediately, a soldier jumped up from the bushes at the side of the road, raised his rifle, and fired a warning shot over my head! Needless to say, I didn't need further encouragement to return to my cab and wait patiently until we were waved on!

As we drove down the road, we could see bloody bodies all around us. Apparently, we had almost been caught in the middle of some kind of armed conflict. Now these precious ones whom God loved were dead—had they known that Jesus died for them? In spite of this sobering experience, we realized that we had been abundantly blessed. God's Word had gone with power all over that division, and we had personally witnessed the Holy Spirit's magnetic influence as thousands of people made decisions for Christ.

Chapter 19

The Submarine Sailor
and the Sabbath

"Do not worry about tomorrow. . . .
Each day has enough trouble of its own."
—Matthew 6:34, NIV

Mike Rowland's submarine docked in Charleston, South Carolina, two weeks before our meetings began. With a two-month leave before his next assignment, Mike had time to attend our meetings. As the meetings progressed, he accepted everything the Bible taught—including the seventh-day Sabbath truth. But Mike was concerned because when his leave ended, he would be flown to the base at Rota, Spain, and from there would begin submarine duty for three months. His job was to sit on sonar watch for four hours every day, seven days a week.

"That's my job, Pastor Kenneth; that's what I'm supposed to do," he said. "So what do I do about the Sabbath? Are you telling me I need to go talk to my commander?"

"Yes, I think that would be a good idea," I replied.

Mike didn't receive the most understanding treatment from his superior officer, to put it mildly.

"I don't care what you say," the commander yelled, "you are going to sit on sonar watch every day—and that's orders!" He added a liberal dose of swearwords for emphasis.

Mike returned to the meetings very discouraged.

"Why don't you make another appointment for both of us to talk to him?" I suggested.

When we arrived at the commander's office, I realized at once that he was in a very foul mood. Along with his colorful and insulting language, he let us know that Mike *was* going to sit on sonar watch—every day. And that was that.

I phoned the Religious Liberty department at our church headquarters. Their lawyers got right on the case and were able to work everything out—the commander was ordered to give Mike his Sabbaths off.

Soon Mike flew to Spain and boarded his sub. But when the first Sabbath came, the commander ordered him to sit for sonar watch. Surprised, Mike stated, "I am sorry, sir, but I cannot do that. Remember, we arranged for me to have—"

"When we surface, you conniving jerk, you will be court-martialed!" the commander shouted, peppering his sentence with more foul language.

Mike couldn't understand what was happening. Why had God not answered his prayer? He was discouraged and fearful for his future, but that only drove him to his Bible with more intensity.

Because of Mike's strong stand for God, as well as his exemplary life on board, several other men on the sub accepted Christ. In spite of that, when the ship surfaced three months later, Mike was taken to Washington, D.C., and court-martialed.

The court ruled that he had disobeyed orders, so he must be disciplined.

"Because your beliefs conflict with your duties," they said, "your punishment is honorable discharge from military service."

His commander faced consequences too. Because he had also disobeyed direct orders to give Mike his Sabbaths off, he would be demoted!

Mike left the military, attended Southern Adventist University, where he studied theology, and then became a Seventh-day Adventist pastor.

A drug deal

Two girls, whom no one seemed to know, also came to the Charleston meetings. After about a week into the meeting, Viki and Carolyn* came to me and asked, "Would you be willing to be a character witness for us?"

"Well, I don't know how I could do that because I hardly know you," I replied. "Why do you need a character witness? What have you done?"

"We've been arrested for selling drugs," they said.

Having learned long before not to react by even raising an eyebrow, I answered, "Well, then, I don't think I could be a character witness for you."

"Well, would you go to court and tell the judge that we've been coming to the meetings?" they countered.

"Sure, I'd be glad to do that," I said.

* * * * *

The judge in the old courthouse wore a stern face. I watched as he took each new case, usually with little mercy. Eventually, he called the girls' names, and they approached the bench.

He said, "If you girls will tell us who you are buying your drugs from, I will let you off—scot-free."

"No way! We're not going to snitch!" they replied. "We can't tell you who we've been buying drugs from."

"Well, then I'll give you a few days to think it over," the judge declared sternly, "and either you tell me who you're buying your drugs from, or I'm going to throw the book at you."

The girls were at the meeting again that night.

"What have you decided to do?" I asked.

"We're not going to tell him."

"He's not playing around with you," I said, genuinely concerned. "If you don't tell him, he's really going to be hard on you."

---

* The girls' names have been changed to protect their privacy.

They just laughed nervously, but when their court date came around, they asked me to go with them again.

When they appeared before the bench, the judge asked again, "Who are you buying your drugs from?"

"We're not going to tell you," they replied.

The sentence was swift and heavy. Carolyn, age twenty-one, was sentenced to nineteen years in prison. Viki, who was nineteen at the time, received a seventeen-year sentence. I watched the blood drain from their faces, and they sobbed as the deputies led them away.

Respectfully, I approached the bench.

"Your Honor, do you realize what you have done?"

"What do you mean?" he asked, obviously surprised at my audacity.

"These girls were coming to Bible-based religious meetings, and I believe there was a possibility of rehabilitating them. But now—"

"We can solve that," the judge interrupted, writing out a note and handing it to me. "They'll let you in to see the girls any time you want to if you use this note."

I went to see them right away. They were sitting in their cells, still sobbing.

"I told you the judge wasn't playing around," I said. "Why don't you just tell him who you've been buying drugs from?"

Nothing seemed to change their minds, as they obviously feared for their lives should they squeal. Finally, in a desperate attempt to save them from their fate, I asked—without thinking it through, "If the people you're buying the drugs from told you it was OK to tell the judge who they are, would you be willing to do it?"

"Sure—like that's going to happen!"

"Would you let me talk to your dealers for you?" *What was I saying?*

"No way."

"Well, how do you know what they'd say?"

The girls discussed this, realizing it was their only hope of seeing daylight for a long, long time. Finally, they wrote out a note and gave it to me.

"When you go out of the courthouse, you'll see a nine-year-old boy standing near the corner. Give this note to him and just wait for an answer," they said.

Strange as their instructions seemed, I took their note and left the courthouse, squinting in the early afternoon sunlight. Sure enough, a young boy was standing exactly where they had said.

"Sonny," I said, handing him the note, "I was told to give you this."

The young fellow glanced at the note, said, "Wait here!" and then took off running. About an hour later, he returned out of breath. "They'll meet you tonight at eleven o'clock on pier twenty-one. Be alone, and don't tell anyone."

How did I get myself into this mess? I'd not had anything to eat all day, but decided that this probably should be a day of fasting and prayer, anyway. Eleven o'clock would come all too soon, and I knew that all the forces of evil had plenty of time to prepare whatever sinister plans they might wish to carry out on that lonely pier.

To say that I was afraid would be an understatement. I never remember being so petrified in my life! But I went to the One who "commanded and it stood fast," the One who states boldly and confidently, "I am the Lord and there is none other."

So at eleven o'clock that pitch-black night, I stood alone on pier 21, my heart pounding, and my knees knocking almost audibly. Had I been presumptuous to venture onto Satan's ground? As I paced, I prayed for protection and wisdom, then for wisdom and protection. After a few minutes, two businessmen dressed in suits and ties walked down to the pier.

"We don't have much use for people like you," they said in menacing tones. Even their body language was threatening. I could envision the revolvers strapped under their jackets.

"I didn't come here for myself," I answered, surprised at the calmness of my voice. "Two young ladies have been sentenced to serve nineteen and seventeen years in prison. But if you would just allow them to say who you are, the judge would release them."

The men laughed and cursed profusely, but, strangely enough, they listened as I pleaded for the girls and their situation. Then they talked together privately for several minutes. After much discussion, they finally wrote out a note.

"Here, take this note, but promise us you won't give it to them for twenty-four hours," they said.

With a sigh of relief and a heart overflowing with thanksgiving, I returned to my room. The note, which they had simply folded, stated that Viki and Carolyn could tell the judge their names—and both men had signed it.

The morning I delivered the note (more than twenty-four hours later, but as early as I was allowed in), the girls couldn't believe what they read! Immediately, they asked the guard to send word to the judge that they would now talk. Later that morning, the courtroom was filled with police officers and detectives—even the walls were lined with uniformed and plainclothes officers. The two girls were escorted into the room.

"Are you going to tell me who is supplying the drugs?" the judge asked.

"Yes," they answered in unison, and Carolyn handed him the note with the dealers' names on it.

As soon as the judge read aloud the names of the two men, a swarm of detectives and officers rushed out—almost creating a vacuum they left so quickly. Of course, the guilty drug dealers were no doubt out of the country by that time.

"I will honor the promise I made to you earlier," the judge said to the girls. "You will be released as soon as we complete some paperwork." So, true to his word, the judge gave the girls their freedom.

And yes, Carolyn and Viki came to the rest of the meetings and gave their hearts fully to the Lord—two more miracles attesting to His amazing grace and power to save!

A voice at daybreak

I'm not one to say, "The Lord told me to do this or that." I believe the Lord has given His Word, and that's where we should look for direction and guidance. But at daybreak one morning in Charleston, South Carolina, I was suddenly wide awake, and a voice said, "Prepare something for television."

I sat up in bed, startled. I was sure I had heard a voice speaking those words, so I took it as a mandate from the Lord to do just that. Our team immediately set out to produce a set of programs.

Of course, we had no equipment for taping, so we returned to Collegedale, Tennessee, and rented equipment and an empty store to record our first television series. These programs were aired free on a TV station in Chattanooga, and we waited for a response. But none came—the programs generated absolutely no response!

I'm still young, I said to myself. *Maybe I just need more experience.* So we prepared another entire series. This time we *purchased* time on television and ran it, but again, there was almost no viewer response. I began to wonder if I'd been seeing things and hearing voices. *Maybe I'm losing my mind,* I thought.

"Let's forget this," I finally said. "Something is definitely wrong here."

A couple of years passed, and we were in Jacksonville, Florida, holding meetings. A young advertising executive, David Eldridge, attended the meetings, and after the second week, he came to me and said, "You need to put these programs on television."

"Thank you," I said with a smile, and then moved on to shake the next person's hand. But David was persistent, approaching me several more times during the meetings with the same idea. Each time I gave him the same answer.

After the meetings were over and I was back home in Collegedale,

Tennessee, someone knocked on my door. It was David Eldridge!

"Come on in, David."

"Hey, Brother Kenneth. I know you think I don't talk about anything else, but I really feel I need to encourage you again to try putting your evangelistic programs on TV."

I explained to him everything that had happened previously and how we'd had no results from our previous attempts.

"You just need some help," he replied. "This is my field, and I'd like to help you."

"Well," I said slowly, "I'll tell you what—you write up a proposal and I'll present it to my board. If they vote it, we'll do it." I was confident there was no way on earth they would vote such a thing, since we'd already produced two series that had seemed failures.

Not to be dissuaded, David wrote the proposal and presented it to our board of directors. I was shocked when they voted to accept the proposal.

So I prepared another entire series, and our team went to Jacksonville, Florida, and worked with David for a couple of weeks while taping the twenty-four programs. Then David managed to place the series on television in Atlanta, Georgia.

The results?

Nothing.

What was happening? We had spent a lot of money and lot of time with very little results, though I was *sure* that I'd been directed by the Lord to prepare programs for television. Was I hearing things? One thing I did know for sure: I would never bother to tape TV programs again. Only later would I learn what God actually had in mind.

Chapter 20

The Dark Before the Dawn

"Don't be afraid; you are worth more than many sparrows."
—Matthew 10:31, NIV

Invitations were coming to the team members to work in various places. Phil and Joey went to the Voice of Prophecy; Benny and Barbara went with the Southern Union. I was invited to be the evangelist for the Southwestern Union—but without a team.

For fourteen years, I had worked with a team, and now, to be without one was devastating. My children were grown and gone, and my circumstances made life seem unspeakably bleak. I'm willing to confide that even an evangelist can become discouraged—and sometimes *very* discouraged. I felt like Elijah—no longer on the mountaintop resisting the priests of Baal, but running through the valley searching for a way of escape.

That's when the Lord sent an old friend, Jim Gilley, to me. He owned a company called Missionary Tape and Equipment Supply in Burleson, Texas. Jim had always been an evangelist at heart who would rather hold religious meetings than do anything else. He often said, "Let's go get a bite to eat," when I was feeling low, so with the aid of some Chinese, Italian, or Mexican cuisine, he supported me through those hard days.

We "talked shop" about soul winning—what worked and what didn't. Jim was the "friend who sticks closer than a brother"—just what I needed. When discouragement almost overcame me and the fire in me burned low, Jim helped rekindle that flame of passion for a dying world. When I had a new idea for evangelism, I knew I could bounce it off him, knowing he would fully understand and give an honest appraisal while still supporting me. We became even closer friends than before.

A debt repaid

During this time, I began a series of meetings in Fort Worth, Texas. Charles and Ellen Klinke, who had worked with our team in Bogotá, Colombia, had moved back to the United States. They offered to work with me in the Southwestern Union if we could cover their living expenses. That was welcome news!

Then one day, the church secretary asked me a question: "Do you know a lady by the name of Mary Russell?"

I thought for a minute. "No, I can't place anyone by that name."

"Oh, she said her name used to be Mary Roberts."

"Oh, yes, I know *her*!" I exclaimed. "She was in the church in McAlester, Oklahoma, when I was a boy. She and her husband, Floyd, were a great help to me when I first began to keep the Sabbath."

"Well, she lives here in Fort Worth, now," the secretary continued. "Her first husband, Floyd, died, and she's now married to a Methodist minister and has become a member of his church."

"Do you ever see her?" I asked eagerly.

"Oh, yes. She lives not far from me."

"Do me a favor and invite her to the meetings," I said. "Tell her I would really like to see her."

Sure enough, that very evening Mary Roberts Russell came to the meeting. Afterward, we had a chance to visit about old times.

"Mary, I'd like to meet your husband. Why don't you invite him to the meeting tomorrow evening?"

The next evening Amos was sitting right beside Mary, and after the meeting I enjoyed visiting with him also. They attended every evening, and about three weeks later, Amos approached me.

"Would you mind stopping by the office at my church tomorrow? I'd like to visit with you some more," he said.

I went to visit Amos the next day, but I was not expecting to hear what he told me. "I've been studying what you've said in your meetings," he said, "and I'm fully convinced that Saturday *is* the Sabbath. I've decided to keep it holy, but haven't talked to Mary about it yet. I don't know what she's going to do, but I've made up my mind that I want to keep God's holy Sabbath. In fact, I'm going to tell my church this coming Sunday that from now on, I'll be keeping the seventh-day Sabbath."

Predictably, his church didn't welcome this new idea, but Amos moved forward anyway, and God blessed him. Of course, Mary was delighted to return to the truth she had once loved. Eventually, Amos became a Seventh-day Adventist minister, and I can't help but think that God must smile at some of our life's experiences. Mary and Floyd Roberts had changed my life when I was a young person, just learning how to be a Christian. Later, I was able to minister to Mary and her new husband, Amos, helping them to come to a deeper understanding of Bible truths.

It was while holding meetings in Texas that I first met Danny Shelton. He told me about his dream of starting a television network to take the gospel to the entire world and how God was miraculously leading. I encouraged him to continue, for we desperately needed a way to send the message of Christ's soon return to the people who wouldn't or couldn't attend meetings. Then, ten years later, I was invited to do an interview with Danny, and we talked of airing our programs on 3ABN. Time had erased the disappointment I'd experienced many years before in trying repeatedly to place these messages on television. But God's providence knows no haste and no delay. He had been working out the details all along—*in His time.*

The television mystery solved

God's hand over His work is often very obvious. San Antonio, Texas, was one city where this was especially true. Through the hard work of Ray Hubbard, evangelism coordinator for the Texas Conference, and the local pastors, we saw large numbers of people coming to the meetings. Both television and newspapers carried the story about the hundreds who were baptized in the San Antonio River—giving us almost unheard-of media coverage.

I began follow-up meetings in one of the churches, and on the second evening, a man with a little home video camera asked if he could videotape the meeting. The moment he opened his mouth, I knew he was not from the United States.

"I guess that would be OK, as long as you're not in anyone's way," I replied.

Carl and Norma Branster were Australian, and each night they set up their little tripod, taping the evening's presentation.

"Do you mind if I take these videos to Australia and show them there?" Carl asked when the meetings were over.

"No, I don't mind at all," I said. Then, as an afterthought, I added with a smile, "Just don't try to put them on television. I've already tried that."

When Carl returned to Australia, he went to see one of the conference presidents.

"I videotaped an evangelist in the United States, and this series is so good, I'd like to show it in one of our churches here in Australia."

"No, I'm sorry, but we cannot allow that," the man answered. The conference president really couldn't be faulted for his decision because he had no idea what was on those tapes.

But Carl wouldn't give up. He knew the conference president on the other side of Australia, so he called and talked to him about it, ultimately obtaining permission to show the series in a little church in the outback. That church had twenty-four members, and they were told they could invite visitors, but that they couldn't advertise with flyers or media—or any such thing.

The first evening the members brought twelve guests, and when the meetings were over, seven individuals were baptized. Carl became very excited and called me from Australia.

"Would you mind if we came back and videotaped your presentation again?" he asked.

"Well, I'm glad it's been a blessing, and no, I don't object," I said.

As we were setting up a few days before our next meeting, a large truck drove up, and Carl jumped out and greeted everyone. "I've come to videotape the meetings," he stated with Aussie enthusiasm.

Indeed he had! I had assumed he would be coming back with his little home video camera, but instead, he had an entire crew—three cameras, a switcher, and all the equipment necessary to produce a professional program! From that series, Carl captured twenty-eight video presentations.

"Would you object if we reproduced these and made them available for sale in Australia?" he asked next.

"I guess that would be all right," I replied, at this point still trying to figure out if I'd been crazy for producing so many television programs years before. I figured nothing much would come of Carl's series, but instead, God used it to begin development of a video and television ministry that has gone around the world. His will was becoming clearer.

Losing Mother

"Hey, Kenneth." I immediately recognized my brother Don's voice on the phone. "Listen, Mother is not doing very well. When she went into the hospital they said she had diverticulitis, but she's just not getting any better, and I thought you'd want to know."

"Of course I want to know, Don. Thanks for calling. I'll see if I can get a flight out right away, maybe tomorrow. What's the name of the hospital?"

I had a pleasant, rewarding visit with my mother. In spite of her many handicaps, she had managed to live alone and take care of herself until the last year or so of her life, when she moved in with my sister, Billie, in Phoenix. We visited together in her hospital room, recalling happier days and times. I thanked her for her steadfast love through the years. We laughed over some humorous times our family had gone through together, and then I prayed with her—and for her.

"Thank you, son," she said, a tear finding its way down her weathered face. A short time later, at the age of eighty-three, she passed away from complications of her disease. She was a faithful Christian woman who had done all she could to help her children follow after God. She was a lifelong inspiration to me.

The prayer in the beauty shop

In 1986, I was invited by the Southeast California Conference to be their evangelist. Most of my previous evangelism in the United States had been in the East and Southwest. Unfortunately for me,

Left to right: Kenneth Cox, Dona, and Gordon Klein

Charles and Ellen Klinke accepted an invitation to pastor in Texas, so once again, I went alone to California.

My first meeting was scheduled in Victorville. Desperately in need of help, I began searching for someone to play the organ. I couldn't afford to hire anyone; all I could do was pay expenses and hope to find someone with a heart for serving God. One lead after another turned up nothing. Finally, someone gave me the name of Dona Klein. I'd never heard of her, but went to her house and knocked on the door.

I was shocked when she invited me in and I found myself standing in the middle of a beauty shop! Dona was cutting hair and giving permanents to three women simultaneously. She invited me to sit down, and right there in front of her clients, I blurted out, "Dona, I need a musician to play for the meetings in Victorville. All I can pay is your expenses for coming to the meetings."

Dona hesitated but a moment.

"Would I be able to bring my own organ?"

We talked about the music, what I expected of an organist, and what type of music I liked. She said she would need to talk to her husband, Gordon, who was assistant administrator of the hospital in Corona.

When Dona told Gordon about the invitation to play for the meetings, she asked if he would be able to take her each evening.

"*Hmm,* let's see—I'd have to get off work early each day," he began slowly. "And with health care employment being so shaky right now, Dona, quite frankly, I'm afraid I might lose my job. I don't know what to tell you."

"Well, I'll pray about it," she said. "Maybe the Lord will work something out."

A few days later, Gordon came home early. As he walked through the door, Dona looked up, surprised. "My, but you're home early!"

"Happy birthday, honey," Gordon replied. "I've been fired. At least I can take you to the meetings now!"

Not exactly the birthday present she was hoping for—but the

Lord's ways are not ours, and He just asks us to walk by faith as He opens or closes those doors.

The moment Dona touched the keys of the organ, I knew that the Lord had answered my prayer. She seemed to sense what was needed at each point of the service, and there seemed to be no end to her repertoire. Her ability to play the organ and piano at the same time made her music distinctly different and beautiful—just what we needed.

Gordon proved invaluable also. He was as helpful in visiting interested people as he was in overall organization. He worked with setting up visitation schedules and keeping computer programs and information current, as well. The two Kleins were a most welcome addition, and it was great to have a team again to share the load.

Pa-Pa's rules

As a result of my frequent travel, I was unable to be a typical grandpa. Though I would have loved to spend more time with my grandchildren, I established a custom of taking each of them for a week's vacation at Disney World in Florida when they turned twelve. At that age, I figure they're generally old enough not to be homesick, and they've not yet become smitten by the opposite sex.

"There are two rules," I told them. "First, if it's wrong, we're not going to do it; and second, if it's going to hurt you, we're not going to do it. Outside of that, it's your vacation."

My second oldest grandchild, Erica, was quite an athletic youngster. After arriving at Disney World, she said, "Pa-Pa, let's go to the water park today."

Pa-Pa had never been to a water park, so I asked, "What do we need to do to go to a water park?"

"Aw, just bring your swimming suit. They've got towels and lockers and everything you need there."

And so it was that we found ourselves at the water park, and after changing into our swimsuits, we splashed through every pool and whooshed down every slide the park had to offer in the first hour. I began to notice there didn't seem to be enough padding on the bottom of my feet, and the pavement was getting hotter by the minute. It wasn't long before I was having trouble walking, and about that time, Erica exclaimed, "Oh look, Pa-Pa! Here's the *perfect* slide!"

We stood in line to take the lift up to the top, but it was a forty-five-minute wait. Erica, being very bright, immediately discovered that we could go around back and *walk* up the stairs, a feat that took only fifteen minutes. Wonderful economy!

By the time we had walked up the stairs for the fifth time, my feet were definitely not in good shape. That's when I instituted my third rule: "If it's going to hurt Pa-Pa, we're not going to do it either."

Chapter 21

Videos, Vacation, and Vladivostok

"Go and make disciples of all nations."
—*Matthew 28:19, NIV*

Steve Gifford, a strong supporter of evangelism, became president of the Southeastern California Conference not long after I began working for them. In an effort to make my work more effective, Steve and the conference officials encouraged me to set up my own corporation and board of directors. That way, decisions could be made by board members from the local conference who understood and supported evangelism.

I established a corporation called Dimensions of Prophecy. Our offices were located in the Southeastern California Conference office building, and the conference president sat on our board, as did several ministers. Service records were maintained by the conference, while the corporation furnished money to pay salaries and rent.

We found this arrangement worked very well, allowing us to exist as a parachurch organization, providing evangelistic meetings for the church. It was during the evangelistic meetings in the Azure Hills church in Grand Terrace, California, that we decided to produce a video series titled *Dimensions of Prophecy*.

Carl Branster from Australia brought in a television crew. We then hired a set designer to give us a sketch of a stage backdrop to make it look professional. This was the series that launched our video ministry and really opened the way for "putting something on television." At last I could see where God had been leading all the time.

Australia and Fiji

Because people seemed intensely interested in understanding the book of Revelation, I decided to produce a second video series, going through Revelation chapter by chapter. Carl Branster insisted that this could be done in his garage in Australia, using a green screen.

So I flew to Australia and stayed with Carl and his wife. With a special green screen behind me, I made my entire presentation. Later, the green background was replaced by illustrations and Bible texts, making it look as if I were standing on a stage in front of massive backdrops. It took six very long weeks to write, shoot, and produce the programs, and we often worked fourteen to eighteen hours a day.

When booking my ticket to Australia, I had been told that I could make one stop of my choice on the way back to the United States. Knowing my work was going to be incredibly intense, I decided to book a stop in Fiji on the way home, spending two days doing absolutely nothing but lying on the beach and listening to the waves. This expectation was like the proverbial carrot dangling in front of a hard-working mule. It gave me hope of a pleasant reward for my weary body and mind, and it kept me going when I could hardly keep up with the punishing, relentless schedule.

So with mingled exhaustion and anticipation, I boarded the plane for the return flight. The flight to Fiji was uneventful, but as I walked down the aisle to disembark in paradise, the flight attendant said, "Welcome to Fiji, Mr. Cox."

"Well, thank you," I said, slightly startled. "How did you know my name?"

"Oh, I've watched your videos," she replied.

I should have realized that conversation was a forewarning of things to come. As I stood in line, waiting to go through customs with twenty-two boxes of newly made videos I was taking back to the States, a voice blared from the loudspeakers, "Would Mr. Cox please come to the front of the line? Mr. Cox, to the front of the line, please."

I didn't move. I had been thinking of how good the warm sun was going to feel on my back, dreaming of the refreshing breezes and the hours of peaceful sleep I was about to enjoy. And besides, I didn't think the page was actually for me. Even if it were, I had twenty-two large boxes with me. I wasn't about to push my way in front of all those people.

It wasn't long before a uniformed man came down the line looking for Mr. Cox.

When he reached me, he said, "Mr. Cox, you need to come up to the front of the line."

"Oh, no," I objected, "I can't do that. I'm not going to carry all this stuff up there in front of all these waiting people."

"Do you need all these boxes with you while you're in Fiji?" he asked.

"No, but I don't have any other place to put them."

"If we stored them until you left, would that be OK?"

"Well, sure, as long as they're in a safe place."

"We'll take care of it. Now you need to go to the front of the line because we have an appointment waiting for you."

What could he be talking about?

My surprise appointment was with none other than the prime minister of Fiji! He had watched some of my videotapes and now wanted to meet me in person. It was a pleasant meeting, but I seriously tried not to glance at my watch to see how much daylight would be left for relaxing in the sun when we were finished.

Then I found out that church members had been busy lining up speaking engagements for me after discovering I would be visiting their beautiful island. After my appointment with the prime minister, I was whisked off to Fulton College, where I spoke to the student body. Several churches managed to get on my impromptu speaking schedule, which also included a trip to the union office, the conference office, various schools, and a worship talk for ministers.

During my two days in Fiji, I spoke four or five times a day and was escorted between appointments and meals. Alas, I never did get to the beach—but somehow God refreshed me anyway.

The advertising problem

As a result of Carl Branster's enthusiasm and videotaping, I was invited to hold evangelistic meetings in the city of Melbourne, Australia, and he asked if he could tape a third series while our team was there.

For these meetings, I was blessed to have my daughter Laura and her husband, Larry, as part of our team. Larry was a tireless worker and excelled at leading song service, singing solos, visitation, and organization. His kindness and thoughtfulness bubbled to the surface in every situation. He was a real gem.

Laura was much like her mother—blessed with the uncanny ability to perceive where help was needed and then doing whatever was necessary, along with loving everyone who attended the meetings. But because Laura and Larry didn't want to raise their children "on the road," they spent only one year with us, which included these meetings.

Australia is a very secular country, and the prevailing idea in evangelism techniques was that the first few subjects of any series had to be either about archaeology or the family. Australians simply would not come out to hear someone speaking on the Bible, I was advised.

Those in charge of arrangements told me I would need to change my subjects for the first few nights. I spent some time praying and thinking about this suggestion. First, it was just not the way I held meetings. Second, I didn't feel right about trying to lure people into meetings without their knowing what the subject actually was. So with a heavy heart I sent back word that if we needed to advertise the meetings as something they were not in order to get people to come, they should probably find someone else to hold them. I just was not comfortable with that approach.

Finally, the coordinators relented. "OK, go ahead and do it your way. But we don't think it will work here."

When we arrived in Australia, I met the pastor who was working with the advertising. "We've got a problem," he began. "We've booked a huge hall that seats two thousand people, but all the tickets are already taken. What should we do?"

"Well, let's hold a second session," I suggested.

In a few days, I heard from him again. "The second session is completely booked now." So we made the decision to hold a third session. In a few days, it was completely booked too.

"What do you want to do now?" the pastor asked again, noting that still more people wanted to come.

"Take the advertising off the air," I answered. The hall was full for all three sessions every evening, the Holy Spirit was present, and many, many people made decisions for Christ.

Carl Branster's crew had videotaped each meeting, and from these, the *Dimensions of Prophecy for Today* series was born.

Asparagus, classic Coke, and the antichrist

While in Australia, we all learned to drive on the "wrong" side of the road. The conference furnished us with a car, which proved to be an interesting challenge since it had no power steering, and the shift stick was, of course, on the *opposite side* from what we were used to. Also, the windshield wiper worked overtime from being accidentally bumped. Our discomfort behind the wheel seemed so opposed to what driving should be that the "contrary car" was soon dubbed "the antichrist."

While I was preaching my heart out, Gordon Klein was doubled over in pain with kidney stones. Someone told him of a sure cure: eat an entire can of asparagus, along with six cans of classic Coca-Cola. He was desperate for relief and wanted to help at the meetings. If only he could just hang in there until he could make it back to the States where he had medical insurance!

So he tried the remedy.

Not only did it *not* work, Gordon wasn't used to having caffeine in his system. Now, besides the excruciating pain, the poor man didn't sleep for days! When Dona took him to the hospital, the nurses gave him something to relieve his intense pain before they even took his name. He spent the entire day in the hospital. Many tests were run, and much medication administered. Finally, the stones passed, but Gordon braced himself for the real pain as they handed him the bill. Quickly, his frown turned to a smile when he saw the total amount due: nine dollars!

God brought success to our efforts, and many dear people were baptized.

Alone in Russia

During the time that the iron curtain was falling, the Lord opened the door for me to go to Vladivostok—a seaport city on the extreme southeastern side of Russia, and one of the main ports for the Russian navy. Carl had managed to get the Melbourne programs translated into Russian, and my plans were to find members of the local Russian Seventh-day Adventist Church who would use them to share the message with others. Our generous ministry supporters had donated funds to purchase projectors, tape players, and copies of the translated videotapes.

Not wanting to go alone on my first visit to Russia, I asked Steve Gifford, the chairman of our board and president of the Southeastern California Conference of Seventh-day Adventists, to accompany me. We were pleased to discover that Alaska Airlines flew all the way, with only one stop in Anchorage to refuel. But knowing no one in Vladivostok, we felt some trepidation. No one would be at the airport to meet us, and neither of us spoke the language. We wavered between the notions that this was a demonstration of pure faith—or utter stupidity.

As we landed, the runway was so rough and filled with potholes that it seemed the plane would shake apart! Steve and I made it through customs without any trouble, but then we suddenly found ourselves on our own. After some searching, we located a man who could speak English and agreed to work as an interpreter for the evening.

We hailed a cab and said, "We'd like to go to the Seventh-day Adventist church." Fortunately, the driver knew where it was located, but when we arrived, we discovered that a Baptist group rented the church a couple days each week. They were meeting that evening, and somehow, it didn't seem the right group to leave the videos with, so we found a hotel and settled in.

Almost an hour later, we reconsidered and decided maybe it would be a good idea to go back to the church, just to see if we could get more information. The church caretaker was at the meeting, and he let us know that the Seventh-day Adventist pastor was out of town for a month, but no one seemed to want to tell us anything else. It was the first time most of them had seen someone from the United States, and we quickly figured out that they didn't know whether Americans could be trusted. We were going to have to wait until Friday evening, when the Adventists would be back.

About eighty members showed up on Friday evening, but not one of them spoke English—not even a little bit! They were all gray-haired and elderly. When we tried to visit after the service without a translator, we were unsuccessful in getting them to understand why we were there. However, one of the couples said they would take us to the pastor's home, for his wife had not gone with him.

High-rise apartments abound in Russia, but they were in a great state of disrepair when we were there. The pastor lived in one of these apartments on the eleventh floor, and, of course, the elevator did not work. The pastor's wife was very gracious and invited us in, but she didn't speak English either. We were able to understand that the pastor was out of town holding evangelistic meetings, and that he wouldn't be back for a month, so we returned to our hotel totally discouraged. Nothing seemed to be working.

Strange dreams

Steve and I talked it over and agreed that we weren't really accomplishing anything we'd come for. Because the airline flew out only on Wednesdays and Sundays, we might as well just go ahead and fly out on Sunday instead of waiting until Wednesday. However, since we couldn't speak the language, we didn't call right away about changing our tickets.

That night I had a dream. A young, dark-haired man with Italian features walked into the room where we were, and a voice said, "He speaks English." The next morning, as we ate breakfast, I told Steve about my dream. "I must have eaten too much for supper," I added.

We both laughed.

"When you went to bed, your mind must have been preoccupied with how much we needed someone to speak English," he said.

Arriving at Sabbath School that morning, we found about 120 people there—all elderly, and, again, no one spoke a word of English. We didn't understand a thing that was going on, but just as the church service got under way, the door opened, and a dark-haired young man with Italian features walked in.

I nudged Steve with my elbow. "There he is!" I whispered. "He's the one I saw in my dream!"

After a few minutes, a Russian woman went over and spoke to him in Russian. He then came and spoke to Steve and me—in English. We couldn't believe our eyes and ears.

"Let's step outside to talk," I suggested.

After we introduced ourselves to him, I asked him if he attended church here.

"No," he said, a slightly puzzled look on his face.

"Then what are you doing here?" I asked.

"I don't know. I attend church on the other side of the city, but I just felt moved to come here for church today."

"*I* know why you're here. The Lord *sent* you," I replied.

Then he told us about a group of young people who met on the other side of the city and invited us to visit them. We left the service and met a dynamic group of young people at the other church. As I explained what we were trying to accomplish, ten of them immediately said they would like to be involved.

Then, to our surprise, the pastor showed up on Monday. He'd also had a dream—about two American men in Vladivostok and that he needed to go home! So he'd caught a train on Sunday, traveled all day and night, and arrived home on Monday morning. We met with him and the youth group and gave them Russian-language videotapes, projectors, VCRs, and training on how to use them. Later we heard that two new churches were raised as the Lord blessed those young people's efforts.

Chapter 22

Day of the Dead

Teaching them to observe all things whatsoever I have commanded you.
—*Matthew 28:20, KJV*

Personal evangelism, one-on-one, is always the most effective way to witness. I have seen this demonstrated over and over again in meetings we've held in other countries, where the church members are not inhibited about asking their neighbors to study the Bible with them or to attend a meeting. A good example of this was the large series we held in Mexico City, Mexico, in October 1994.

Taking a taxi anywhere in Mexico City is quite an experience! They travel at sixty miles an hour through downtown traffic, speed down one-way streets the wrong way if that's where they need to go, and ignore traffic lights and right-of-ways. Horns honking, drivers yelling, and cars bumping each other are the "traffic solvers." Few, if any, vehicles are free of dents.

After some of our team members expressed concern to their aggressive taxi driver, he suggested, "If you don't like our taxis, take the subway." We thought that was good advice and discovered that the subway was really quite nice.

Our evangelistic meetings were held in a large permanent tent that normally was used as a dance hall, and church members brought visitors by the hundreds. Because the meeting place was not located in the finest part of town, a concrete wall with broken glass embedded along the top surrounded it.

Our rearview screen and curtains made a nice backdrop, giving us a place to meet and pray each evening before going out on the platform. With security as a serious concern, we hired a couple of strong young men to stay overnight, protecting our equipment.

One of our meetings was held on the the Day of the Dead, an important festival in Mexico City. They call it *Día de los Muertos,* and a number of superstitions surround the event. After the meeting that night, we rode the subway back to our hotel, but as soon as we walked into the lobby, I realized I'd forgotten to get my keys off the organ, where I put them each night while I preached. I told the others to go on to bed, and I would go back alone for my keys.

Arriving at the tent area, I found the entrance shut and locked. I rattled the metal gates and yelled, *"Hola,"* trying to get our security guards' attention, but there was no response. I walked around the concrete wall surrounding the tent, found a place I thought I could climb over, and then jumped down onto the main tent ground. A small lightbulb, intended to chase the darkness away, cast eerie shadows instead. I could barely see, but managed to get backstage behind the screen. I called out again and then shouted—but no one answered. Knowing exactly where I'd left my keys, I finally just reached through the curtain. But instead of keys, my hand grabbed the sleeping night watchman's leg.

Arms and legs flailed for a bit, until a very white Mexican face with very large, dark eyes stared at me. I was glad at that point that I didn't understand very many words in Spanish. Keys in hand, I returned to the hotel, chuckling over the evening's excitement. I was pretty sure my young friend didn't get any more sleep that night.

When the security guard saw me the next evening, all he said was, "Boo."

Because I didn't speak Spanish, my ability to communicate with the people one-on-one was limited. I had to depend on the ministers and laypeople to work with those they were bringing. It was delightful to see the Holy Spirit at work.

A thoughtful church member had built a large baptismal tank on a flatbed truck. When this was delivered to our site, it was accompanied by a large tanker truck full of hot water! We had a wonderful baptism, and our time in Mexico City was extremely rewarding. The people were warm, loving, generous—and responsive to the gospel.

Gone fishing

Back in the States, I remembered a lesson I had learned as a boy. We had just moved to Oklahoma when some of the neighbor boys invited me to go fishing with them. I knew nothing about fishing, but the boys showed me how to get a good fishing pole, line, cork, weight, and hook. Then they taught me how to bait the hook and where the best places were to fish.

One day I was sitting on the bank fishing, when a man sat down beside me and began baiting his hook. However, he didn't just have one hook, he had two! *That's smart,* I thought. *His chances of catching fish are twice as good as mine.*

From then on, I always fished with more than one hook at a time. Later, I saw a fishing boat with fishermen pulling in a long line with hooks every few feet.

"What are you doing?" I asked.

"Oh, we're trotline fishing," they answered.

Another time, I saw more fishermen in a boat drawing in a net filled with fish. I then realized there are many ways to catch fish—and it's the same with "fishing" for men and women to lead to Christ. Sometimes people can see only one way to do a thing—their way. But the Bible says God has *a thousand ways,* as I soon learned.

My schedule was full, the program was growing, and our video ministry was gaining momentum. One day I was working in the California office when I received a telephone call.

"Pastor Cox, I'm Freda Shultz from Lancaster, Ohio. I'd like to use your videotapes to follow up some literature evangelism leads."

"I see. So how can I help you?" I asked.

"Well, I can't afford your videos, so I'd like to ask you to loan them to me."

"Hmm," I mused. "Freda, tell me something about yourself."

She explained she had been a minister's wife and a Bible worker. Her husband had died while they were working in Alaska. She had then moved to Lancaster and wanted to help the small church that had only fourteen members.

"Well, Freda, I'll loan you a set of tapes, provided you will keep me informed every month on how it's going."

"I'll be happy to," she exclaimed, "but I'm going to need more than one set of tapes."

"Oh, how many do you need?"

"I could use five sets."

"Are you sure you can handle that many?" I asked.

"Absolutely."

So we sent five sets. In a month, Freda called and said things were going great. She told me about several people she was studying with, and then she said, "I could use more tapes."

"How many more would you like to have?" I asked in shock.

"Well, I could use five more sets."

I sent her the tapes, and we mailed out ten thousand cards in her city, asking people if they'd like to watch the videotapes in their home. Freda followed up the card responses, and soon was studying with ninety people a week—while working full time as a nurse at the local hospital!

The Holy Spirit blessed her efforts, and Freda's little church grew. Today, it has more than a hundred members as well as a church school, and she continues to use video sets (which are now DVDs). As the video ministry grew, I asked Freda if she would train churches on how to use the DVDs in preparation for future evangelistic meetings.

It's surprising what one person can do when following the directions Christ gave us to "seek ye first the kingdom of God." When people say they don't have time to give Bible studies, it is often because it's just not high on their priority list. Those who have a love for people, along with a love for God, cannot keep from telling others about Jesus Christ.

God opens doors, and by faith we are to walk through

Maddy Couperus

them. I again felt the great need of vocal help since my team had been dissolved. To find someone who was willing to go on the road for ten months out of the year—and live out of a suitcase—seemed so remote. Finding a person who would sing as worship and not as performance was a tall task. But with God all things are possible.

We were conducting a camp meeting at Pacific Union College when we met a woman named Maddy Couperus who had a marvelous voice, just the right type for evangelistic meetings. But I had never heard of her before. So I decided to ask her to come and sing for a weekend at one of our meetings. This would give us an opportunity to get better acquainted and to see how she would fit in with the team. She turned me down twice before she finally consented.

Then, *after* she joined the team, she found out that I wanted all our vocalists to know all their songs by memory! Maddy was aghast! Her first song, "I'll Rise Again," contained four rather difficult verses, so she sat in a corner until she had them down pat. When necessary, she could even learn the words and music while I was preaching—a God-given talent!

Maddy had one of the clearest and loveliest voices I'd ever heard.

She knew how to touch the audience and could sing an appeal song like an angel. She worked with us on the road for twelve years.

Friendships often open doors for much needed help. Back in the days before Maddy gave her heart to the Lord, she would sing in nightclubs. She had a close friend by the name of Diane Loer who would often go with her to hear her sing. But of course, with Maddy's conversion, she stopped singing in the clubs.

When Maddy began to sing for us, Diane would come along. But she didn't believe in God, and made it very clear that she wanted nothing to do with religion! She would sit up front in the audience with Maddy, putting down her magazine only when Maddy got up to sing. The Bible says, "Cast your bread upon the waters, for you will find it after many days" (Ecclesiastes 11:1, NKJV). It seemed like I was casting it out on a rushing river! But God is true to His Word. Little by little, we began to see a nick in Diane's armor, and the day came when she surrender her heart to the Lord.

Another friend of Maddy's was Lindi McDougal. She had multiple sclerosis and was confined to a wheelchair. Because of their friendship with Maddy, Diane became acquainted with Lindi and eventually became her caregiver.

They've been volunteering now for the past ten years, taking care of all the material used during the meetings, such as sermon outlines, call cards, offering envelopes, and books. They also keep the mailing list up-to-date. But that's not all. Diane and Lindi have been dubbed "the A-team" because they never leave until everything is finished.

Grand Ole Opry star

A request for an evangelistic series came in from Medford, Oregon, a lovely town in the southern part of that state. The area churches there were active and friendly, and the response from opening night on was good. The pastor and laymen at that church worked hard together, faithfully visiting those who came to the meetings, and God blessed with a baptism of more than a hundred people.

Roy Drusky, from the Grand Ole Opry, came to Medford to sing. On a day off, we decided to take him on a boat trip down the Rogue River. There were probably fifteen or twenty people in the boat, and the man conducting the tour found out that Roy Drusky from the Grand Ole Opry was with us. As we pulled up to the wharf, the tour guide stood up and announced, "We are happy to have Ron Driskle, from the Grand Ole Opry with us today!"

Everyone clapped and said hello to "Ron." Being a sweet gentle person, Roy just smiled and returned their greetings. Perhaps no one but us knew the difference. Roy and his wife, Bobbye, were great friends and were always an asset to our ministry.

No snow

You'd think if someone were going to hold a meeting in Alaska, they'd want to do it in the summertime. But, no, we received an invitation to do a series in Anchorage starting in November! Many people are gone in the summer, have too much company, or work late in their fields or offices during those long days, they explained. But winter nights are long, and something different, such as our meetings, would have a certain appeal.

While people in Alaska look forward to snow so they can enjoy their snowmobiles and winter sports, what we didn't need was for it to snow so much that they couldn't get to the meetings! We had been told that it could snow as much as four or five feet during that time of the year, so the churches decided to have an all-night prayer meeting, pleading for God's blessing and asking Him to hold back the snow.

God does hear and answer prayer. While we were there during the months of November and December, snow barely dusted the ground. In fact, the town folk became a bit unhappy because they couldn't use their snowmobiles!

We tried a new schedule and conducted one meeting at 1:30 P.M. and a second at 7:00 P.M. This made attending the meetings convenient for older folks who couldn't get out after dark as well as for those who worked at night. It has proven true that when the pastors and laymen work together, God blesses, and Anchorage was no exception. A large number of people were baptized.

Clothesline out back

We were constantly receiving requests to have the videotapes translated into Spanish, so when the invitation came to hold meetings in McAllen, Texas, I decided to have each night's presentation videotaped. We would have a Spanish translator, José Guillen, one of the local pastors, stand beside me on the platform. Over the years, I've had a lot of good translators, but none has ever worked with me as well as José. He never got ahead of me, and he was never behind. I knew my thoughts were getting across to the people because they laughed and "amened" in all the right spots. José was truly sent of God!

But each evening, as we came to the meetings, I noticed something strange behind the auditorium. I asked if there was anybody living back there because I always saw a full clothesline of wet clothes hanging out to dry.

"Oh, no," they responded. "Those clothes belong to the people who wade the river from Mexico each night to attend your meetings. They bring another set of clothes held over their heads to keep them dry, and every day they change into their dry clothes from the day before."

I didn't ask any more questions! God blessed with more than two hundred baptisms in that series.

The day that never should have been

Without question, the enemy of souls harasses us, hoping to discourage and confuse. Such was the day that should never have happened.

We left for the Ontario, California, airport at 5:45 A.M., in plenty of time to catch our flight to New Orleans for an organizational meeting. We stood at the counter for an hour and a half while the agent tried to find our reservation, and finally we missed our flight. Later, the airline finally found them, but for some unexplained reason, the transaction had never been completed.

Next, we were shuttled to Los Angeles' LAX airport by van—at eighty miles per hour! The driver was stopped for speeding, but the kind policeman didn't write a ticket. Arriving at the airport, we literally ran to the gate, only to discover that the plane had left two minutes earlier. So they put us on another flight, but after waiting on the tarmac for thirty minutes, our plane was determined to be unsafe for flying.

We were finally put on a flight that arrived in New Orleans twenty minutes before our 7:00 P.M. meeting—minus our luggage!

The book of James tells us that we need to allow patience to do its work so we may become more like God. Frustrations remind us that victory is not given to the weak and fearful, but to those who go forth in faith—knowing the Lord is omnipotent and will open the way before them.

Chapter 23

In the Loop

"Lo, I am with you always."
—Matthew 28:20, NKJV

In 1997, the Voice of Prophecy board of directors invited me to work as their evangelist. This put us in the organized church work at a place where evangelism was front and center, which definitely had its advantages. The Dimensions of Prophecy Corporation was absorbed by the Voice of Prophecy, and, as one condition for making the move, the entire team was put on salary.

The transition went smoothly, except for finding housing in Simi Valley. The price of homes in that area was totally out of reach. In fact, I searched for a year and never found anything I felt I could afford. I didn't realize that the Lord had other plans.

I was asked to conduct the Net '97 satellite evangelistic series out of Tacoma, Washington. It was my first Net meeting, and I had much to learn. My friend, Don Gray, was an invaluable help.

From this series, we produced a video set called *Hope Beyond 2000*. These were translated into French to be used overseas, primarily in Africa. Our idea was to train African laymen to go out to the villages with the gospel. Each trained layman received a set of tapes, a projector, a VCR, and a generator to use where electricity was not available. Duane McKey, a strong supporter of global evangelism, was responsible for getting this accomplished under the auspices of Adventist

Global Mission. Hundreds of African laymen were trained, and untold thousands were brought to the Lord through their work. Africa was the next place the Lord opened up for our team.

Lusaka, Zambia

Pastor Mulendema, president of the Zambia Union Conference, extended an invitation for us to hold meetings in his country. He was a young father of seven children. At a camp meeting held in the countryside prior to the evangelistic meetings, we ate with his family in a hut made of elephant grass. There were no facilities except a hand pump for water in the middle of the encampment. His wife cooked our meal on a little fire in front of the hut. As we ate, she insisted that we sit on stools while she sat on the ground. Later, Pastor Mulendema bounced his baby on his knee as we visited. I looked forward to working with this man of God because of his vision and desire to get the work done.

Sadly, the very next day this good man was in a serious automobile accident on the way to his office and was pinned inside his car. Emergency

Translator and Kenneth, preaching to thousands at camp meeting.

medical help was not available, and he bled to death. A pall of sorrow hung over the church organization in that country as our series began. The void in leadership left many loose ends, even though others tried hard to tie things together. Needless to say, the loss was traumatic for us all.

The capital city of Lusaka had been chosen for the meetings, but no auditoriums were large enough to accommodate huge crowds in this city of more than two million people. So an outdoor series was planned, and Gordon Klein rented a soccer field on the edge of the city. I wanted to use a video projector to illustrate the presentation each evening, but wondered how large a screen we would need in order for the estimated ten thousand people to see it. We quickly realized we would essentially be erecting a wind sail that might very well sail off into the night! Finally, we decided on a plywood screen twenty feet high by sixty feet long, braced by four or five telephone poles! Larry Claridge, a builder from College Place, Washington, volunteered to oversee that project, and I appreciated him from the start.

Lights, sound, video projection, platform, ushers, greeters, music, children's programs, and many, many more details had to be arranged long before the meetings actually began—so the entire team went over early.

Fifty thousand kwacha

After the major details had been worked out and the organizational wheels had begun to turn, Gordon, Dona, and I decided to do a bit of sightseeing at Victoria Falls. We rented a car, and to get there quickly, I drove with a heavy foot all the way. We very much wanted to get across the Zimbabwe border before midnight when it would close, so we'd have plenty of time for sightseeing the next day.

However, because of enormous potholes and other road conditions, we didn't make it in time, and had to spend the night on the Zambia side. Seeing a motel that advertised hot running water, we thought it wise to stop and get rooms for the night.

The floors in our rooms were covered with paste wax that had never been buffed, so things were a bit slippery. The next morning we were disappointed to find that our bath water was cold! Inquiring at the front desk, I reminded the gentleman of what his sign advertised. In just a few minutes, a man came running down the hall with a five-gallon pail of hot water—so we *did* have hot "running" water after all.

On our return trip Gordon was driving, as he fancies himself a more "reasonable" (i.e., slower) driver. As we approached a tiny village, we spotted some downed trees far ahead. Gordon was barely creeping along when a couple of soldiers in uniform stepped out from behind the trees and stopped us. One soldier took his place in front of our vehicle, and they all had machine guns drawn on our car.

"You were speeding!" one of the soldiers said sternly.

Gordon hadn't seen any speed limit signs, but he knew he hadn't been driving fast. Under the circumstances, however, he decided it was best not to argue.

"Will you take a credit card or a check?" he asked.

"No! Cash only! That will be fifty thousand kwacha" (about US$35), the soldier said, without even asking for Gordon's driver's license or identification of any kind. We all sent up fervent prayers for divine protection.

We paid the fine and went on our way, noticing that the trees had been dragged across the road to keep tourists from driving past the soldiers.

Sheet on the barn

The week before the meetings were to begin, while the rest of the team was busy with on-site preparations, I asked if I could go out in the bush and watch a layman conduct a meeting using the video projector and generator. So one evening my hosts and I climbed into a Jeep and headed out into the twilight. After a while, the Jeep left the road and started down a dirt trail. We were now literally in wild country and total darkness as we bounced and jounced down the dirt path illuminated by the jeep's dim lights.

After about thirty minutes of our jolting ride, we saw a faint light in the distance. The light turned out be a lightbulb hanging from a tree. On a sheet that was tacked to the side of a barn, someone was showing the *Hope Beyond 2000* videos we had videotaped the year before.

A layman was translating and preaching in his dialect to about two hundred people sitting on the ground. When the meeting was over, we talked to him and to another lay preacher who told us they had baptized 120 people that morning, and soon would be baptizing forty more. Between the two of them, they had started ten new churches in the past year and a half!

The dedication of those men of God was incredible; however, their needs were also great. Having heard that African pastors were greatly in need of clothing, we had collected twenty good suits and brought them with us, along with shirts and ties. A few dollars took care of having all the suits altered to fit, and we were grateful for the chance to minister to their needs.

God's amplification

Twenty thousand brochures were printed for church members to give out in their Lusaka neighborhoods. They were beautiful brochures— a little too beautiful! Church members were very willing to knock on their neighbors' doors and show them the handbill, but they would not give the brochures away because they wanted to keep them!

Our sound equipment was adequate for between three and four thousand people—but not for an entire open soccer field. Though we tried to get a larger system, or at least more speakers, all the delivery dates were projected at least five weeks into the future—long after the meetings would be over. So we used what we had.

Opening night saw fifteen thousand people in attendance, and the numbers multiplied, until by the end of the first week our attendance

Evangelistic meeting in Lusaka

was running as high as forty thousand! The soccer field was completely filled, and people were sitting on the ground, while the bleachers overflowed with those who had come early to get a seat. We suggested starting the meeting at 7:00 P.M., but local people wanted to start it at 5:30 P.M. because they wanted to sing for an hour and a half!

Several hundred children sat right in front of the platform. I thought to myself, *I'm going to be in trouble with all these children sitting right down front. They'll be restless in twenty minutes, and they'll start playing and making noises.* But, surprisingly, the children sat still for the entire two-and-a-half-hour service without a peep—quiet as mice and never unruly. And it wasn't because they were shy! One evening, while the local minister of music was leading the singing, a little four-year-old girl got up on the platform and began following him around. After a while, he stopped and handed her the microphone.

"My name is Swahili Dube, and my memory verse is . . ." Her sweet little voice quoted the Bible text perfectly. Then she added, "What do you say, church?"

"Amen!" the crowd roared.

And the singing? Oh how those people could sing! That hour-and-a-half song service was filled with choirs, quartets, solos, and great hymns. The music was worshipful, dignified, and mostly a cappella because musical instruments are rare. After the meetings were over, the organ we had brought with us stayed in Africa.

Each night people came with pencil and paper to take notes, and when I made the invitation, hundreds came forward, giving their hearts to Jesus Christ. By the time I arrived every evening, long before the meeting began, fifteen to twenty groups of up to fifty people would be in the bleachers. The local pastors were giving them instructions concerning their decisions to follow the Lord.

There was a bar next to the soccer field where the meetings were held. Normally people sat outside, and very loud music blared out all evening as they drank heavily. But while the meetings were being held, the patrons sat and listened quietly to the sermons. The Lord must have impressed their hearts, as no distracting music was ever heard, and by a miracle of amplification, all forty thousand people were able to hear the message clearly!

The witch doctor

One night as I was preaching, a bloodcurdling scream raised the hairs on the back of my neck! I remembered hearing that in Africa people had been killed by wild animals in the darkness. The screaming continued from somewhere very close—perhaps fifty feet away.

The congregation, enthralled by hearing God's Word, was seemingly unperturbed about whatever was going on, so, with a silent prayer, I left the problem with the Lord and the deacons while I continued to preach. The screaming continued for perhaps thirty minutes—but at least I had the microphone!

Later I discovered that a female witch doctor had given her heart to the Lord, but the demons inside her were resisting wildly. Having experience with such things, the local church pastors and elders had taken her to the prayer room located at the rear of the platform, calling upon God to cast out the demons. As we left the meeting that night, it was evident that God had heard and answered their prayers, for there in the darkness, a little fire still smoldered where they had burned all her witchcraft charms. She found complete release in her deliverance and praised God for His mercy.

The lost lunch pail

With such large crowds coming to the meetings, just keeping the place clean was a challenge, so we hired some men to clean the grounds. The day after the last meeting, I thanked them and paid them for their work. Not far away, I noticed a forlorn boy and girl, probably six to eight years old, looking on.

"Who are these children?" I asked.

"They came to the meeting last night," one of the men explained. "Their mother sent their lunch with them, but when they went home last night they forgot their lunch pail, so their mother sent them back in the dark to get it, telling them, 'Don't come home until you find it!' "

The children had searched all night long, and the cleaning men had looked everywhere, too, but to no avail.

"Here, take this money," I said. "Go to the store and buy them a lunch pail and send them home."

One day, as I spoke to the workers, someone asked me, "Pastor, since you have gone into full-time evangelism, is there anything you miss about regular ministry?"

"Actually, there are two things I miss," I replied. "As evangelists, we don't get invited to workers' meetings in a local conference because we are not local pastors, so we miss out on the fellowship with other ministers. Also, because we holding meetings all the time, we seldom have an opportunity to partake in the Communion service."

Without my knowledge, those dear pastors planned a Communion service the last Sabbath at the soccer field. It was an awesome sight to see thirty thousand people washing each others' feet and partaking of the Lord's Supper—a true taste of heaven.

In spite of the devil's many efforts to halt the meetings in Zambia, thousands accepted Christ and were baptized. What a thrill it was to work where God's Spirit was so evidently being poured out.

The loss of a friend

In March 2000, I visited Harold (H. M. S.) Richards Jr. in the Glendale Adventist Hospital. It was heartbreaking to see such a big, booming, dynamic man reduced to such frailty. Harold had always strongly supported evangelism and truly desired to see the Lord's work move forward. I greatly admired his leadership.

We received word that Elder Richards had succumbed to cancer the following month, just as we were starting a series in Albuquerque, where as a young intern, I had been under his leadership years before. What a loss to the church, to the Voice of Prophecy, and to me personally! The best we could do in his honor was to throw our hearts into winning Albuquerque for Christ—the city in which we have held more meetings than any other.

A very close call

I was also asked to do a Net meeting in Chicago that year. That city has always held great interest to me because it was the place of my birth. I'd flown into Chicago several times for one-day meetings, but had not spent any significant time there since moving to Oklahoma as a child, so my anticipation ran high.

We started out from California, driving east in our motor homes. Just out of Victorville, California, in a fifty-five mile per hour speed limit zone, my motor home was hit from behind by a tractor-trailer rig doing seventy miles per hour! The motor home shot down the road like a pool ball struck by a cue stick, but by the mercy of God, I careened within the confines of the road and was able to avoid hitting anyone else. I finally brought the motor home to a halt, pulling over on the shoulder. Trembling, I climbed out to survey the damage. Far behind me, the semi lay in the ditch, its front torn completely off. Then I realized that the entire back of my motor home was missing!

Gordon and Dona had been traveling ahead, but when they did not see me in their rearview mirror for some time, they became concerned. Doubling back, they discovered the accident scene. After answering the highway patrolman's questions, filling out some paperwork, and arranging for my damaged vehicle to be towed back to Pomona, I gathered up my Bible, my sermon outlines, and some clothes. The Kleins took me on board with them, and we all thanked God that no one had been seriously injured—including the truck driver, though quite a dent had been made in our plans. More than just a little shaken, I rode on to Chicago with the Kleins to begin the meetings. Once there, I revisited some of the old familiar places. I went to the corner of Harrison and Damon streets, where my family had lived. Even though much had changed, memories flooded my mind. It felt strange to walk those streets and relive the sights, sounds, and smells of my childhood, realizing how much influence those early days had on my life.

The Midnight Cry

The Lord led us to a good location for the meetings—a large, beautiful ballroom in a hotel turned assisted-living home. The ballroom worked nicely for 3ABN to broadcast the meetings. Attendance was good, and the uplink for the meetings each evening was thrilling, especially when we began receiving e-mails and faxes from various countries telling us how much they were enjoying the presentations.

A big disappointment, however, was the struggle with all the electrical problems. One problem resulted in the programs not being translated into Spanish as planned. However, we rejoiced with the angels over the thousands around the world who accepted Christ and followed Him in baptism, both during and right after the series, which we called The Midnight Cry.

But even while our Chicago meetings were in full swing, major changes were taking place at the Voice of Prophecy following the death of H. M. S. Richards Jr. The board of directors and the new leadership wanted to try some new things. Halfway through our series, I was notified that they were letting our team go. From Chicago, we were already committed to go directly to Wisconsin to hold five ten-session meetings back-to-back during October and November. I arrived back in California near the first of December and immediately went to the Voice of Prophecy office. Thanks to Walter Arties and Marshall Chase, we worked out satisfactory separation agreements that everyone could live with. By the end of the year, we were no longer working for the Voice of Prophecy.

Chapter 24

In the Path of the Storm

Even unto the end of the world.
—Matthew 28:20, KJV

With no headquarters and no name for our ministry, we rented a dark little basement in Loma Linda, which we dubbed "the dungeon." This is where our evangelism equipment was kept, and we worked out of that cubbyhole for some time, continuing to book meetings and move ahead.

We had named the series of Net meetings held in Chicago The Midnight Cry, and we decided to just call our new organization The Midnight Cry Ministries. Soon a problem surfaced, however—another ministry was already using the name, and, understandably, they protested our use of the name. So we had to change the name on all the videos. At that point, we decided on Kenneth Cox Ministries. At least, no one else was using *that* name.

Once again, we decided to move our living quarters. Because of the nature of our ministry, we needed to live within thirty to forty miles of an airport. We also needed homes with driveways long enough to park our motor homes. Unable to find affordable housing in California, we decided to look in the middle of the U.S. That way, we wouldn't be far from home, regardless of which coast we were working on. Fortunately, our homes in Grand Terrace sold quickly, and eventually both the Kleins and I found suitable places not far from Nashville, Tennessee.

About the same time, we realized that the "dungeon" in Loma Linda was becoming too small. After much prayer and searching, we made a down payment on a property for a ministry building in Yucaipa, California. The reason we kept our office in California was that moving all our furniture, supplies, and equipment would be a major expense, not to mention the fact that we would have to hire and train new help too.

We began holding ten-session meetings, beginning on Friday evening and ending on Saturday evening the following week. This schedule included two services on Sabbath. We decided that we could probably do fourteen such series a year. Soon we discovered that it made for a crazy and unbelievably difficult schedule, but from 2002 through 2005, that's exactly what we did—one meeting right after another. It seemed we could barely get things torn down before having to set them up all over again. Grouping several series together in the same area of the country helped, but during those four years we crisscrossed the country several times.

During our meetings in Yucaipa, California, we began clearing land for our new office. At this time, Jerry and Beverly Brass, who had retired from church work, began helping us. Jerry took over the task of booking meetings—a job at which he excels and continues to do even now. Bev provided expertise and support in answering correspondence, and continues her work with our team as well.

That same year we moved into our new office building, and thanks to God's blessings and the faithful support of our donors, we have not been in the red or had to borrow money. Our ministry team is supported mainly through donations as well as through sales of our DVDs, since the offerings taken during the series usually cover only the meeting expenses. We've often had only a few hundred dollars in the bank, but the Lord has always provided—even during the construction of our building. The Lord brought us an experienced contractor, Stan Nelson, who did a wonderful job of construction, and we walked by faith, building only as we had the money—but progress never stopped. When our building was finished, it was completely paid for. Praise God!

The rest of the story

While holding meetings in Houston, Texas, we realized that we badly needed a truck to haul our equipment. My friend Blake Chanslor contributed a twenty-four-foot box van, but now we needed someone to drive it. When Dona offered, Gordon and I both laughed, but we finally decided that Dona would drive my motor home, Gordon would drive theirs, and I would drive the truck. We were now a three-vehicle caravan.

One day as we cruised down the road in Oklahoma, a car passed me. The driver waved like a long-lost friend, and though I recognized no one in the car, I smiled and waved back. The car went on ahead a little way and then slowed down. As I went around them, they waved again and motioned me to pull over. Because they appeared to be a family and probably not dangerous, I pulled over to see what they needed. And there on the side of the road, I learned the rest of a story that had begun long before.

At the start of my evangelism career in Oklahoma, I'd been holding meetings in Shattuck when a church member died in Muskogee. The family asked me to conduct the funeral, but since it was too far to drive there and be back in time to preach that night, the family had hired a pilot (who was not a church member, or even a Christian, for that matter) to fly me to Muskogee.

As we flew that day, I was able to share the gospel with the young pilot, and he accepted Jesus Christ as his Savior. Now, twenty years later, he recognized me when he passed me on the highway. He just wanted me to know that he was still serving the Lord! What a joy!

I drove that truck for three years, and while conducting a camp meeting at Sandia View Academy outside of Albuquerque, I invited Blake Chanslor to take a look at the truck he had donated. He had never seen it, and as we were talking about it, he asked me how it drove.

"It's a good truck," I replied, "especially for a preacher."

"What do you mean?" he asked.

"Well, it shakes the devil out of ya."

Blake hired a driver for us that day, and I've never driven the truck since.

But finding someone to drive a truck is not an easy job. The driver would need to be a rare breed of man—dependable, flexible, and without roots—but the Lord had it all worked out. We were holding ten-day meetings in Delaware; while we were in Dover, a fellow by the name of Chuck Allgaier showed up. He enjoyed the meeting and asked us where we were going next. We told him we would be leaving soon for Salisbury, Maryland, and sure enough, when we started those meetings, Chuck was there.

After we finished, he asked me where we were going next, and I told him we were headed to Fredrick. Awkwardly, he asked if we would mind if he attended that meeting as well, and I assured him it was fine. As the Frederick meetings were coming to an end, Chuck approached me once again.

"I think I'd like to go with you to your next location, if you could use some help," he offered.

"Well, Chuck," I said, "we're going to Sacramento, California, next, and we could certainly use the help, but I'm afraid I can't pay you anything."

"Oh, that's no problem," he answered. "I pay my own way."

But without our knowledge, Chuck began to have second thoughts about his decision once he thought things over a bit. At the next evening's meeting, we were having a drawing to give away some gifts, and Chuck decided to place a fleece before the Lord.

"Lord," he prayed, "if You really want me to go with them to Sacramento, please have them draw my name." Of course, as God would have it, his name was the first to be drawn out of the basket!

Chuck proved to be a very valuable worker, and I realized he would be a good person to drive the truck and set up for each meeting. Soon we were able to hire him, and he has worked with us for the last ten years.

"I know you!"

In early 2005, I received an invitation to hold meetings in Guam. They asked me to fly out to go over all the details with them. I told the sponsors how the program worked and what the costs would be to get our team and equipment there, plus the additional expenses of renting an auditorium, printing handbills, etc. After the Guam Mission looked over the figures carefully, they decided they simply couldn't afford to hold the meetings.

I left Guam with the understanding that there would be no meetings, but a few weeks later, I received a call from one of the doctors in Guam, along with one of the pastors.

"We've talked this over," they said, "and we've decided we should go ahead and have the meetings. The mission doesn't feel they can do it, but we want to move ahead with plans anyway."

Again I went over the costs with them.

"Do you think you can afford to have the meetings?" I asked.

"Yes," was their solid answer. So we began to make arrangements.

The Guam meetings were coming up when I received word that the pastor had rented the field house at the University of Guam—a large gymnasium seating about six thousand people. Interestingly, the total Seventh-day Adventist membership on the entire island is only about seven hundred, scattered among seven churches.

They asked our team to come two weeks early to conduct a Week of Prayer at the medical clinic and to hold meetings at the prison.

I was on a plane out of Los Angeles flying to Guam for the meetings when I got up to get a drink of water and stretch. As I walked past the flight attendant, she said, "I know you!"

"You do?"

"Oh, yes, I've watched your videos," she replied, adding that she was busy at the moment, but would like to stop by and visit later on.

When she came by my seat, she told me how the night before, in her hotel room, she had asked the Lord for a sign to help her come back to Him.

"When I saw you, I knew the Lord was answering my prayer," she exclaimed.

As she told me her story, I found out that she and her husband had lived in Hawaii, and some friends had shared my videos with them.

"We enjoyed them so much," she said. "In fact, we accepted the message and were baptized as Seventh-day Adventists. We went to church there in Hawaii, but then my husband's employment changed, and we moved to a little town in Texas that had no church, and we didn't search for another. Now I see how that was a very bad decision," she added.

I enjoyed the opportunity to eat lunch with her in Hawaii and to talk with her about spiritual things. I'm also thankful that she recommitted her life to the Lord as the result of that divine appointment.

The Catholic chaplain

During our first week in Guam, we held meetings every day at the prison as well as at the medical clinic. When the meetings were over, the Catholic chaplain came to talk to me.

"Since you're going to be in Guam for a while, why not come back and talk to the prisoners several times each week?" he asked.

So we arranged for me to continue coming three times a week throughout our stay. After a few speaking appointments, I said, "Chaplain Brown, I've been speaking here several times, and one of these times I'm going to have to talk about baptism."

"That's OK," he replied.

So I spoke about baptism—and more than twenty inmates made their decision to be baptized.

"Now, Chaplain," I said, "what are we going to do? These men want to be baptized."

"Well," he answered, "I can't sprinkle them because they know it's not biblical. But we have a baptismal tank here. I guess you'll have to baptize them."

A few days later, I said, "Chaplain, I'm going to have to speak to them about the Sabbath."

"Now is that something your church teaches, or is that taught in the Bible?" he asked.

"Oh, it's definitely in the Bible," I replied.

"Well, then, I guess you can speak on it."

So I preached about the Sabbath, and a number of men made decisions to begin keeping it holy. We baptized them, and a little church was born right there in the prison.

Typhoon

After arriving in Guam, we discovered that our meeting place had been rented for a boxing match on Friday night—just before we opened on Saturday night. Protesting that there was no way we could get it all set up and ready for the meeting without having access to the auditorium on Friday made no difference. The contract had been signed, so we decided to open our meetings on Sunday night, instead.

On Wednesday before the meetings were to begin, news came over the radio that Guam was in the path of a typhoon that was projected to hit the island on Sunday evening about six o'clock. The announcer said there would be winds up to 135 miles per hour, with at least eight inches of rain. Such a storm would, of course, close down the meeting and bring much damage in its train.

On Thursday, the governor came on the air and declared a curfew for Sunday. Everything must be boarded up by noon, and no one was to be out after that. In addition, all of our advertising signs would have to be taken down.

Our team and the churches began praying fervently.

"We have some good news," the radio announcer declared on Friday. "It looks like the typhoon is not going to hit our island directly.

Instead, it will miss us by fifteen or twenty miles. But we will still have winds in excess of one hundred miles per hour and six to eight inches of rain."

I asked all the churches to come together again in prayer on Sabbath morning, asking God to intervene.

About 3:00 P.M. that afternoon, the announcer came on again.

"We don't know what has happened, but the typhoon has turned and is now going a totally different direction."

"Keep me alive"

Our five-week evangelistic series opened Sunday evening without any wind or rain—and with an attendance between three and four thousand. From the beginning, I was seriously concerned about the finances. Renting the field house at the university cost forty-six thousand dollars, and with all the other expenses, such as shipping our equipment and the cost of transportation and advertising, the cost was now over one hundred thousand dollars. Toward the end of the meetings, the doctor and the pastor came to me with a confession.

"Pastor, we're so sorry, but we don't have enough money to pay for your shipping, air fare, and other costs. You will get your money eventually, but it's going to take us a while to raise that much."

"Then let me make a special call for the offering on Friday evening before we close," I suggested.

Something else was also happening that the audience didn't know about. During the meetings I began having trouble breathing, so I went to the Guam Adventist Clinic. I was very impressed with the doctors. They checked me thoroughly and then broke the news that I had congestive heart failure and that my heart had gone into atrial fibrillation. At almost the same time, Gordon began having physical problems too.

My doctor said, "Look, Brother Cox, we want to send you home immediately. There simply are no medical facilities on this island capable of giving you the care you really need."

My thoughts raced. We had rented the field house of Guam University at great expense, and several thousand people were coming to the meetings every night.

"I don't see any way possible for us to close the meetings down," I told my doctor. "This is an attack by the enemy of souls. So, I'll tell you what—you keep me alive through these meetings, and when they're over, I'll fly straight back home."

Through the grace of God—and excellent medical help—that's exactly what both Gordon and I did.

On Sunday night, during the last week of meetings, I told the audience exactly what our expenses had been and what the money was being used for.

"Would you please pray," I asked them, "because we don't have enough money to pay the expenses for these meetings." Then I added, "Now when I'm asking you to pray, I'm not asking you to pray about what your neighbor can do, but about what *you* can do. We'll take a special offering on Friday evening."

I asked Gordon before the meeting on Friday to let me know how much the offering was when it was counted so I could announce it at the close. As the meeting ended, Gordon came to the platform.

"How much was the offering?" I asked eagerly.

"I don't know yet," Gordon replied. "We're still counting."

That evening the congregation gave enough money to pay all the expenses of the meetings—*with money left over*. And, more important, 350 people were baptized, increasing the island's membership by 50 percent.

The next morning, on a plane headed to California, I began to reminisce. *I don't know what the future holds as far as my heart is concerned. And I don't know what the Lord has in mind concerning my ministry. But one thing I do know—He's granted me a wonderful life, filled with blessings unimaginable.*

In California, I received immediate medical help and began to improve. But Gordon's X-rays showed a tumor on the left side of his brain just above his ear. The doctor said it was glioblastoma, a very aggressive cancer, and one of the most difficult to treat.

"Mr. Klein," he said gently, "I'm sorry to tell you that your prognosis, at best, is that you have only two to three months to live. If we operate, and you take chemotherapy and radiation treatments, you might live fifteen months."

What do you do when you've been knocked to the ground, as far as your health is concerned? You get up. And when it looks dark, you move ahead, even when you cannot see.

Gordon was anointed at the 2005 General Conference Session by Pastor Don Schneider, our friends Pam and Jimmy Rhodes, Dona, and me.

God in His mercy and love gave Gordon five more years to minister to souls who were in need of the Lord. As Paul said, concerning his companions in the gospel, their names are written in the book of life. Without a doubt, Gordon's name will be there, along with many others he brought to Christ through the years. Gordon lost the battle with cancer and passed away December 28, 2009. He was faithful unto the end, fought the good fight of faith, and now awaits the call of the great Life-Giver. For twenty-four years, he was my right arm, a kind and gentle man that I loved as my brother. I will greatly miss him.

The unsafe motel

The next year was a blur as we conducted numerous meetings in various states. While we were preparing for a meeting in Ventura, California, Denny Kukich, a good friend and frequent volunteer helper, asked Dona to find him a place to stay, so he could fly to Ventura and help with the meetings. Dona inquired about a certain motel and was told it was a good place to stay. However, when Denny arrived, he discovered that it was not such a nice place after all. He even felt a bit unsafe.

As he was coming out of his room one morning, he spoke to Arnie, another fellow who was also staying there. Denny invited Arnie to the meeting, but he made an excuse, saying that he couldn't come. The next day, Denny invited him again, and again Arnie turned down the invitation. Then a day or so later, their paths crossed again.

"You know, Denny, I think I'll go to your meeting tonight," he said, and so he came to the meeting that evening—and every night thereafter. At the end of the series, he was baptized, and Denny is positive it was through Divine Providence that Dona booked him at that particular motel—for Arnie's sake.

Chapter 25

Jesus Is Coming!

"As it was in the days of Noah, so it will be
at the coming of the Son of Man."

—*Matthew 24:37, NIV*

Every individual who has come to Christ through our ministry (or any other) has a unique and special story. Each one is a testimony of God's love and mercy, and I have been able to tell of only a very few in this book. Our team members thrill anew with each decision for Christ. No work on earth compares to bringing someone to the foot of the cross and seeing satanic fetters fall away. Retelling the beautiful story of God's amazing grace to people hungry for assurance brings a satisfaction like no other. We are always aware that the result is not from our skill—it is *totally* God's work.

We did not know

As never before, the certainty of an imminent and catastrophic end for this old world looms large. These are exciting times to be alive, and though my physical strength will inevitably ebb, my desire to spread the gospel has increased in urgency. A favorite sermon illustration concerns this end-time topic: Matthew 24:37 says, "As it was in the days of Noah, so will it be at the coming of the Son of Man." Then verse 39 says that they "knew nothing . . . until the flood came" (NIV). The people in Noah's day did not know that the end was upon them. And so it is now.

Dona and I were scheduled for a speaking appointment and organ concert in Sacramento, California. Gordon figured that we could all spend a few days vacationing and sightseeing—entirely free from pressures for a change. He arranged for us to fly to Seattle, Washington, and then take a boat to Victoria, British Columbia, where we would spend two delightful days resting and enjoying the change in scenery.

Gordon was especially fond of trains, so on the return trip, we planned to take the boat back to Seattle, spend the day sightseeing, and then catch the evening train back to California. We would get a sleeper car back to Sacramento, arriving in plenty of time for our appointments.

After returning to Seattle, we checked into our hotel rooms. In the morning we enjoyed a leisurely breakfast, had our devotions, then Dona gave us each a haircut. Now we were ready to go sightseeing.

"We really don't want to haul our luggage around all day—why don't we see if we can check it in at the station?" I suggested.

"Good idea," Gordon agreed, so I called the train station.

"We're scheduled to take the nine forty-five train this evening to Sacramento, and we were wondering if we could check in our luggage this morning so we don't have to carry it with us all day," I said.

"What's the number of the train you're supposed to catch?"

I told him. There was a brief pause, and then he said, "Mr. Cox, your train doesn't leave tonight—it leaves at nine forty-five this morning."

I glanced at the bedside clock. It was 9:40.

"Uh—is the train ever late?" I asked.

"Never," he replied.

We grabbed our luggage, rushed to the front door of the hotel, and hailed a waiting cab. As we jumped in, we told the driver to get to the train station as fast as he possibly could.

"What time does your train leave?" the driver asked.

"Nine forty-five," we responded.

"It's *already* nine forty-five," he said.

Even though we were in downtown Seattle, the taxi tore off at seventy miles per hour all the way to the depot, never catching one red light the whole way—about a ten-mile trip. As we pulled into the station, we could see the train still there and the conductor standing at the door staring at his watch. I rewarded the taxi driver handsomely as we screeched to a halt. Jumping out of the cab, we grabbed our luggage and ran.

"Can we make it?" we shouted.

"As long as the train doesn't move," the conductor yelled back, as he opened the luggage compartment door. "Jump in."

We threw our luggage—and ourselves—into the baggage compartment. The conductor slammed the door shut, leaving us in utter darkness as the train took off like a bullet. We sat there, stunned, thanking the Lord that we'd actually made it.

"It was totally a miracle of grace," Dona declared.

"Absolutely," we agreed as we found the door that opened into a passenger car.

Just as the people in Noah's day did not know when the storm, relentless in its fury, would come, Gordon, Dona, and I did not know that the train was leaving that morning. Missing the train would not have changed the fact that it was gone, even though it was our "last chance" to meet our appointment.

Left to right: Chuck Allgaier, Kenneth, Lindi McDougal, Diane Loer, Dona, and Gordon

Not knowing is a dangerous condition to be in and can result in eternal loss. If you do not know Jesus Christ, please search the Scriptures until you find God's amazing love and promises for you. Reach out to Him, surrender to Him, and He will assuredly answer and guide you.

With this conviction in my heart, I have to keep telling the old, old story to anyone and to as many as I can. The Lord opened up the door for us to begin a series on 3ABN called *Give Me the Bible*. This would give us the opportunity to reach millions with the message. I have felt for a long time that we needed to focus on some of the main subjects in Scripture in greater detail. This series gave us the chance to broadcast five live presentations each month on subjects such as salvation or the Second Coming.

I had prayed that the programs would reach the hearts of the people, but I wasn't prepared for the response. Letters and phone calls poured in from people of all faiths expressing their interest in God's Word. Hearts were given to the Lord, and many stepped out in faith and began keeping the Sabbath. Even those who had opposed the truth for many years finally accepted the message. Dr. Gordon Matthews of Barbados is one of these.

Dr. Matthews was a well-known evangelist on the island, but had actively opposed the Advent message for years. As a young man, he felt the call of God on his life and began preaching and holding evangelistic meetings for the major Sunday keeping churches in Barbados. He distinguished himself as a preacher and a student of God's Word, but when he occasionally ran across Adventists, he dismissed them as a cult. He even used his radio program, which was heard islandwide, to belittle the Adventists, whom he felt were not following the Bible.

But God had a plan for his life, and when 3ABN became available on cable, he began watching our programs. He says he was impressed with their simplicity and clarity, and that the messages touched his heart and conscience. As he studied the Bible in this new light, marvelous truths opened up to him. He recommitted his life to the Lord and was rebaptized, joining the Seventh-day Adventist Church. At eighty-five years of age, Dr. Matthews says his only regret is that he never really investigated and accepted the Sabbath truth earlier in his life.

Chapter 26

What Have I Learned?

We also bear record; and ye know that our record is true.
—3 John 12, KJV

Now here I am, a seventy-five-year-old man. Some young people will think I'm so past my prime as to be laughable; yet some might be willing to hear what an evangelist of such "advanced age" deems to be the most important lessons he's learned in life (sort of like how folks listen to a dying man's last words). So here's a bit of what I've learned.

About salvation

God has *great* big plans, and I am only a minute speck in them. The only reason I figure into His picture at all is because of Jesus Christ. Without Him I am nothing. We are told that because of Jesus, we can come boldly to God's throne of grace to present our needs and requests. But we need to keep the relationship clearly in mind. We are not going to present some brilliant plan to change the universe, or that God will say, "Thank you, My child. We could never have done it without you!"

He is so far ahead of us that our ideas and plans are as baby talk. In our lowly, sinful condition, the best we can hope for is to surrender our pride and arrogance and accept His Son. Then, by His grace, and the work of the Holy Spirit, He will teach us to live as His sons and daughters.

When it comes to salvation, there is nothing we can do. We cannot add to it or improve it. It is totally and completely the work of God. He is the Potter; we are the clay. Our responsibility is to be pliable in His hands by surrendering day by day to His will and to accept what He says in His Word for our lives. We can't say, "That goes against what I was taught," or, "That doesn't matter," or, "That's not what I want to do." He is God and He will make the decisions.

It took forty years in the wilderness for Moses to understand that he was a nobody. It took three years in the Arabian Desert for Paul to find out he didn't amount to anything. And unfortunately, it takes many of us a lifetime to realize that God is totally Sovereign—we are privileged—oh, so privileged—to merely work in His vineyard.

Can you imagine that God gives *humans* the opportunity to be in His kingdom? The sacrifice of Christ that made it possible for us to be there should take away any and all selfishness and strife.

About reputation

When we work for the Lord, because it counters the devil's plans, he will attack furiously, and it will often be in the area of our reputation. We need not defend our reputation, despite the temptation to do so. If we have done what is right, we can leave it all in His hands. Ultimately, His opinion is all that matters.

About working together

It's wonderful to have individuals working with you whose hearts beat with the same compassion for saving souls and who recognize God's leading in their lives. I will ever be grateful to my team and board members for their love, support, and devotion to the cause of God.

All individuals should be free to think and pray for guidance and to follow the Lord's leading. Some team members have worked with me for a little while and then left because they felt the Lord calling them to work on their own or with another ministry. This is the way the work expands, and I thank God for their faithfulness to Him.

I've been blessed with team members who knew how to organize and get things done. Many concepts that have been incorporated into my ministry sprang from ideas that a team member had. They knew how to put their shoulders to the wheel and get the work done, even when things were hard. Sometimes they jokingly referred to me as Pharaoh, demanding "more bricks," but as we worked together, they understood that the work they were doing was every bit as important as mine.

About waiting

Learning to wait on the Lord has been one of the hardest lessons for me to learn. It is His timing, His enabling, that makes His work successful.

When He is leading, the waters will part, and the way will open before us. That doesn't mean there won't be challenges. We aren't fighting against mere flesh and blood, but against a spiritual foe who will do all within his wicked imaginings to hinder our work. So watch for the flow. When God leads, obstacles will fall on the left and the right, as He makes our paths straight.

About trust

Once I settled the question about waiting on the Lord, I had to learn the lesson of trust, or what we call faith—for trust is faith. I had to quit trying to handle life's circumstances and, instead, stand on His Word. This required learning to trust even in the areas of food, shelter, clothing, and reputation.

Faith in the Lord doesn't require that we understand. Scripture says, "Faith is the substance of things hoped for, the evidence of things not seen" (Hebrews 11:1, KJV). This was a lesson I had to learn concerning the death of my wife Marilyn. I could not put it all together in my mind. The children needed her, and so did I. We had put our hearts and souls into the ministry, so surely He would heal her. I prayed night and day, pleading with the Lord, but it was not to be. Why not? I still don't know, and in this old world I will never know—until He comes and makes it plain. When I accepted Him, it was for good or ill, and I chose to put it all in His hands. I came to the realization that God loved me and He loved my children, and I chose to trust Him.

Do I have questions? Oh, yes. I still do. But I have the assurance that they will be answered by and by.

Would I do it all over again?

I would do it again, in a heartbeat. Leading men and women to Christ is where ultimate joy is found. I've enjoyed a wonderful life here and anticipate a glorious life in God's soon-coming kingdom. No more tears; no more heartaches—oh, yes, and to be with Jesus!

Has it been hard? Of course. Leaving family behind, not having any roots, being a stranger in my own community and church—there have been some untold sacrifices. But nothing can take away the pure joy of watching the Holy Spirit convict and convince the hearts of God's precious children, pointing them to His kingdom! To share this with men and women has been a compelling passion.

✦ INSPIRING STORIES FROM INSPIRING SPEAKERS ✦

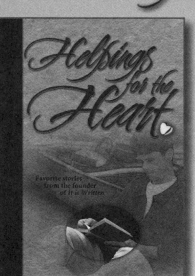

Helpings for the Heart
by George Vandeman

George Vandeman understood that stories had the power to make people stop, listen, think, and even laugh. Stories can change lives. Over the course of his remarkable ministry, George Vandeman used stories to draw people to Christ. *Helpings for the Heart* is a wonderful selection of the best stories and illustrations he used in his ministry.

Paperback, 128 Pages
ISBN 13: 978-0-8163-2272-5
ISBN 10: 0-8163-2272-4

Keep On Keeping On
by James W. Gilley

Often humorous and very personal, from 3ABN president Jim Gilley, *Keep On Keeping On* is a balm for the bruised and a pep rally for the depressed. When you feel like throwing in the towel, *don't*. Instead, put your hand in Jesus' hand and keep on keeping on!

Paperback, 160 Pages
ISBN 13: 978-0-8163-2059-2
ISBN 10: 0-8163-2059-4

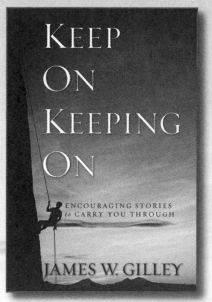

Pacific Press®
Publishing Association
"Where the Word is Life"

Three ways to order:

1	Local	Adventist Book Center®
2	Call	1-800-765-6955
3	Shop	AdventistBookCenter.com

T H E
O P E N
D O O R

A Novel

Floyd Skloot

Story Line Press

1997

© 1997 by Floyd Sk..

l rights reserved. No part of this book may be reproduced in any
m or by any electronic or mechanical means including informa-
n storage and retrieval systems without permission in writing from
the publisher, except by a reviewer.

Published by Story Line Press, Inc.,
Three Oaks Farm, Brownsville, OR 97327

This publication was made possible thanks in part to the generous support
of the Andrew W. Mellon Foundation, the Charles Schwab Corporation
Foundation and our individual contributors.

Cover Art: Room in New York, Edward Hopper, 1932 oil on canvas, 29 x 36
in., Sheldon Memorial Art Gallery, University of Nebraska.

Book design by Chiquita Babb

ACKNOWLEDGMENTS

I would like to thank the Oregon Arts Commission for a literary fellowship,
and the Villa Montalvo for a writer's residency which assisted me in the com-
pletion of this work. I also want to thank Lawrence B. Salander, whose lifelong friendship, support and example are a steady source of inspiration.

My wife Beverly's love and support have once again enabled me to complete this book.

Portions of this novel appeared in the following magazines: *Changes,
Confrontation, Glimmer Train Stories, Midstream* and *Voice*. I am grateful to
their editors.

Library of Congress Cataloging-in-Publication Data

Skloot, Floyd.
    The open door : a novel / by Floyd Skloot.
       p. cm.
     ISBN 1-885266-48-0
  1. Jews—New York (State)—New York—Fiction. I. Title.
    PS3569.K577O64 1997
    813'.54—dc21
                                        97-25392
                                          CIP